CHILD CARE

CHILD CARE

MARJORIE EBERTS, Ed. S.
AND
MARGARET GISLER, Ed. D.

THIRD EDITION

New York Chicago San Francisco Lisbon London Madrid Mexico City
Milan New Delhi San Juan Seoul Singapore Sydney Toronto

The *McGraw·Hill* Companies

Library of Congress Cataloging-in-Publication Data

Eberts, Marjorie.
    Careers in Child Care / by Marjorie Eberts and Margaret Gisler.—3rd ed.
        p.   cm.
    Includes bibliographical references.
    ISBN 0-07-148211-3 (alk. paper)
    1. Child care workers—Vocational guidance.   I. Gisler, Margaret.   II. Title.

    HQ778.5.E24 2007
    362.71'202373—dc22   2007010431

To Aerin, Kyle, Ella, Alden, and Lily—the newest members of our families

1 2 3 4 5 6 7 8 9 10 11 12 13 14 15 16 17 18 19 20 21   DOC/DOC   0 9 8 7

ISBN 978-0-07-148211-0
MHID   0-07-148211-3

McGraw-Hill books are available at special quantity discounts to use as premiums and sales promotions, or for use in corporate training programs. For more information, please write to the Director of Special Sales, Professional Publishing, McGraw-Hill, Two Penn Plaza, New York, NY 10121-2298. Or contact your local bookstore.

This book is printed on acid-free paper.

CONTENTS

like • What being a salesperson in a children's retail store is like
What being a creator of children's products is like • What working
with children and computers is like • Still more jobs exist

CHILD CARE CAREERS—AN INTRODUCTION

Japan celebrates one day a year as "Children's Day." Those who choose a career that lets them work with children will find that every day on the job is a special day. What's more—it's an important career choice because it actually affects what children will do in the future. Tomorrow's leaders, teachers, doctors, judges, salespeople, astronauts, and computer programmers will all remember how those who worked with them as children helped them achieve their goals. A child who is in school today will be president of the United States or prime minister of Canada tomorrow. Some will even be Nobel Prize winners. A few will make new discoveries that will impact the lives of everyone, as the automobile and computer did in the twentieth century. The future happiness, health, and welfare of all children depend greatly upon the help they receive from all those who have careers involving their care. This book deals with those careers.

In the twenty-first century, parents will remain their children's main caregivers. They will, however, receive more help than ever before in raising their children because the majority of them are employed outside the home. The old African proverb—"It takes a village to raise a child"—is as true today as it was hundreds of years ago. Parents are being directly assisted in caring for their children by child care workers in their own homes, child care centers, and preschools. Teachers from kindergarten through college are helping children obtain the formal education essential to surviving in our modern world. Health care professionals are keeping children healthy and helping them recover from illnesses or injuries.

When children have serious social or emotional problems, psychologists, psychiatrists, counselors, and social workers are there to help them.

Parents in this new century are looking to professionals not only for help in caring for, educating, and keeping their children healthy. They are also involving those who have careers that will lead to the enrichment of their children's lives. Today's parents especially want their children to acquire sports and recreational skills such as soccer, karate, swimming, gymnastics, basketball, and horseback-riding from professionals. They are also seeking to expand their children's creative skills by giving them lessons in the arts. After school and in the summer, parents are looking for youth organizations that can provide their children with such activities as camping, crafts, and scouting. Parents also expect professionals to entertain their children in movies and videos and on television, and at birthday parties, restaurants, and amusement parks. Because parents are seeking so much help in the raising of their children, more careers than ever before are associated with children. In addition, there are careers associated with the creation, manufacture, and sale of products used primarily by children.

SO MANY CHOICES EXIST TODAY FOR CAREERS ASSOCIATED WITH CHILDREN

Yes, the traditional child care careers—teachers, nannies, and pediatricians—are still out there and remain great choices. But these careers have changed and become even more exciting with all the new technology. Every one of them has been touched in some way by the computer revolution—from the way people find jobs to how they handle them. Then there are all the new careers, such as life specialists making children's hospital stays more pleasant, instructors working with preschoolers in sports and music classes, online advisers giving children homework advice, and computer experts devising innovative websites for children. This book will explore both traditional and new careers involving the care, well-being, and interests of children. Here is a bird's-eye view of some of the careers described in this book:

Working in Child Care Centers

About 70 percent of children under the age of six have working mothers. About half of them are being cared for in child care centers. The employment picture for those who wish to work in these centers is extremely rosy as there are more than a hundred thousand centers, and this number is expected to increase. Most child care centers are nonprofit and are run by school districts, community agencies, religious institutions, and other local organizations. Businesses are also starting to operate child care facilities for their employees. Although some for-profit child care centers belong to regional and national chains, most are owned by individuals and families. The major downside to a career working in child care centers is that the pay is generally low and few benefits are offered; however, this is beginning to turn around as more state and federal money is being designated for child care.

Caring for Children in Your Home

There are more than three hundred thousand licensed and unlicensed in-home child care businesses in the United States. In Canada, 30 percent of the young children—not being cared for by their parents—are in home-based child care centers. The owners of these businesses are able to work with children without leaving their homes. They have established profit-able businesses that are less complicated to operate than many other businesses. Of course, it is not possible to set up an in-home child care center without complying with certain governmental regulations, and it is also essential to develop a business plan. In addition, owning a child care business involves such tasks as obtaining insurance, buying supplies, advertising services, and hiring employees. Furthermore, it is essential to be knowledgeable about child development, as a program must be cre-ated that will help each child develop socially, emotionally, physically, and mentally.

Working as a Nanny

Mary Poppins is probably the world's most famous nanny. While nannies are not expected to fly through the air as Mary did, they have many of the same duties that she had. They are almost totally responsible for the care of their charges. Nannies plan the days for the children in a family and supervise most of their activities. Nannies may live inside or outside the family home and typically work long hours and have weekends and holi-days off. The demand for nannies is far greater than the supply. The job does require training, and most professional nannies have babysat, worked in child care centers, attended nanny school, or have a background in early childhood education.

Working as a Babysitter

Babysitting is a less formal job than being a nanny. Babysitters usually go to a home to help working parents or parents who want a night out or a short vacation together. Babysitters may also babysit children in their own homes. Babysitting is often an intermittent or part-time job. A babysitter typically watches the children of just one family at a time. However, two or more families may get together to hire a sitter. Wages are generally paid on an hourly basis. There is a tremendous demand for babysitters, especially those who have proved reliable. For teenagers, babysitting is an excellent way to enter the job market as well as to gain experience that will prepare them for other child care careers.

Educating Children

The teaching profession is the largest in the world. From Aristotle to this year's Teacher of the Year, the task of teachers has always been to help other people learn. Teaching as a profession has developed largely since the 1800s when teacher-training schools opened in western Europe. Teachers in preschool and Head Start (see Chapter 3) programs have usually been required to take several courses in early childhood education. Kindergarten, elementary, and middle school teachers, however, normally have bachelor's degrees. A career in teaching is an investment in the next generation.

Working with Children in Sports and Recreation

Many of today's children are filling their leisure time with organized sports and recreation activities. They are eager for sports instructors to teach them sports skills or how to become more adept at a sport. Their interest in sports ranges widely from the traditional, such as tennis, swimming, and basketball, to the less well known, such as archery, karate, and canoeing. Children also seek recreation through some form of play, amusement, and relaxation. Recreation workers help children learn how to use their leisure time effectively. They work at recreation and parks departments, at summer camps, and with civic, social, fraternal, or religious organizations.

Keeping Children Healthy

Health care professionals have the opportunity to exercise the compassion they feel for children in a meaningful way. They diagnose illnesses, perform medical examinations, and treat children suffering from injury, disease, and mental health problems. At the same time, they advise parents on their children's diet and hygiene and on preventive health measures. Most careers involving the health care of children require special training and licensing. Certain health care careers, such as pediatric cardiology and child psychiatry, demand years of postgraduate training and education. Health care is a hot job market. The number of jobs in this area is expected to expand by 30 percent between 2007 and 2014.

Ensuring the Welfare of Children

Children can be the victims of poverty, family problems, and abuse. Some children join gangs, commit crimes, and do not attend school regularly. Choosing a career in child welfare or juvenile justice is an opportunity to make the world a better place for children who find themselves in unfortunate situations and to rehabilitate those who exhibit antisocial behavior. Such careers require individuals who are mature, objective, and extremely sensitive to children and their problems. Social workers, police officers, juvenile court judges, court referees, and child advocates are concerned with ensuring children's welfare. They find jobs in child welfare departments, police juvenile bureaus, adoption agencies, crisis intervention services, schools, hospitals, clinics, and social service organizations. According to the Bureau of Labor Statistics, jobs associated with providing services and assistance to children and their families to improve the social and psychological functioning of children will have significant openings between 2007 and 2014.

Introducing Children to the World of Arts and Entertainment

Visual artists, dancers, and musicians share their expertise with children as they teach them these arts. Just as many children are attracted to sports, many are also drawn to learning how to play musical instruments, dance, and draw pictures. Children gain pleasure from acquiring skills in the different arts, and they also enjoy being entertained. Clowns and magicians amuse children, and so do actors in children's theaters and on radio and television programs designed for children. Careers in entertaining children are for those who want to bring enjoyment to children while satisfying their own desire to be in front of a camera, microphone, or audience.

Additional Careers Working with Children

Jobs helping and caring for children are found just about anywhere there are children. At a library, children's librarians help children select books. Artists may concentrate their careers on capturing images of children on canvas or in stone. Children's book illustrators bring authors' tales to life. Salespeople in children's shoe stores fit children in the correct shoes, and clerks at toy stores help children choose toys. In churches, youth ministers tend to the spiritual needs of young people. An amazing variety of jobs exists for those who want careers working with children.

FINDING THE RIGHT CHILD CARE CAREER

Deciding to work with children leads to making a decision on which career to choose. There are so many choices. Assessing one's individual aptitudes can make the career choice much easier. The following questions can make it simpler to find the career area relating to the care and well-being of children that is most appealing to you.

1. Am I primarily interested in teaching children?
2. Is the health care aspect of caring for children my major interest?
3. Do I want to work directly with children, or would I rather work in a job related to their care or well-being?
4. Do I prefer to work with a specific age group, such as newborns, toddlers, preschoolers, or school-age children?
5. Do I prefer working with both children and their families?
6. Would I rather work with one child, a few children, or a group of children?

7. Do I want to work in an office, child care center, home, clinic, or hospital?

8. Do I want to establish my own business?

9. Would I like to supervise other employees?

10. Do I want to work in the private or public sector?

11. Do I want to work for a profit or nonprofit business or organization?

12. Would I prefer to work for a small, medium, or large business?

13. Am I willing to get training or a college degree in order to pursue my career interest?

14. Am I willing to read constantly to keep abreast of what is happening in my career field?

15. Do I truly like children so much that I want to devote my career to their care and well-being?

THE CURRENT AND FUTURE OUTLOOK FOR JOBS

Parents are now using a veritable village of workers to help them raise their children, ranging from the traditional teachers and health care professionals to the more recent counselors, sports coaches, and online homework gurus. In the future, parents are likely to rely even more than they do now on other caregivers to nurture, teach, guide, and entertain their children. This trend will result in more jobs in almost every area dealing with the care of children. In fact, it is anticipated that employment of workers in almost every career associated with caring for or teaching children will increase much faster than the average for all occupations through 2014.

LEARNING MORE ABOUT CHILD CARE CAREERS

An excellent source of information for most careers related to child care is the *Occupational Outlook Handbook*, compiled by the U.S. Department of Labor. Consult this book before making vital career decisions. The book gives information about working conditions, employment opportunities, training required, advancement opportunities, earnings, and future job outlook for most types of work. It can be found in libraries, bookstores, and online at www.bls.gov/oco. Canadian readers will find that the

Career Handbook gives information on duties, skills, interests, aptitudes, educational requirements, and work settings and can be found online at www23.hrdc-drhc.gc.ca. And of course, there is the Internet, which can be surfed for an abundance of information ranging from job opportunities to career preparation to résumé writing to expected earnings.

C H A P T E R

2

LEARNING ALL ABOUT CHILDREN

No matter what career is chosen in child care, it is so important to know exactly how children develop. Individuals directly involved in the care of children, such as child care center workers, at-home family caregivers, nannies, babysitters, teachers, doctors, and dentists, need to be very aware of the general guidelines describing when children typically acquire important skills. When should a baby begin to respond to commands or recognize his or her name? How old does a child have to be to understand cause and effect? When should a child be able to use a spoon or to skip? How old does a child have to be to acquire the idea of acceptable behavior or know how to use a tissue? Knowing the basics of child development is the way caregivers know what their charges should be able to do and lets them choose appropriate activities for them. It also lets them see if the children are developing skills in an age-appropriate way.

Others in careers associated with children need to understand children's development. The creator of a new toy, for instance, uses this information to assign an age range for its use. The dance teacher is aware of what type of dances young children can learn. The magician knows what tricks will enchant the audience in different age groups. The author knows what type of book will appeal to a three-month-old or a three-year-old child. The following skills checklists were developed by the authors and first published by Meadowbrook Press in *Ready for School? What Every Preschooler Should Know.*

CHECKLIST OF EXPECTED LISTENING SKILLS

Birth to fifteen months
- Reacts differently to loud and soft sounds
- Looks to see where sounds come from
- Responds to human voices
- Knows the difference between angry and happy
- Identifies different speakers
- Likes to listen to self babble or talk
- Knows the sounds that favorite toys make
- Imitates sounds
- Recognizes own name
- Understands names of familiar people and objects
- Begins to respond to commands
- Understands more words than can actually say
- Associates sounds with objects (drums, rattles)
- Understands "no"
- Enjoys listening to poems and stories

By two-and-a-half years
- Likes to be read to
- Has favorite storybooks
- Listens to short stories
- Recognizes the words for common objects
- Recognizes the names of people
- Identifies body parts
- Understands the position words *on, under, in*
- Understands simple questions
- Understands simple commands
- Listens for the meanings of words, not just sounds
- Listens to adult conversations
- Repeats sounds, words, and phrases

By five years
- Appreciates stories, poems, and music
- Listens to stories without interruption
- Recalls story facts

- Retells a simple story in sequence
- Tells the meanings of words heard in a story
- Repeats simple nursery rhymes
- Follows simple two- and three-step commands
- Understands and follows rules
- Recognizes common sounds (animals, cars, running water)
- Distinguishes between loud and soft sounds
- Identifies beginning sounds of words
- Hears the differences between similar sounds
- Identifies rhyming sounds
- Copies simple rhythmic patterns (clap clap—clap clap)
- Imitates common sounds (dog, siren, horn)
- Hears soft whispers and understands the words
- Identifies unfamiliar words and asks their meanings
- Tells the meanings of simple words
- Understands the position words *in front of, behind, toward*
- Understands most adult sentences
- Repeats a series of five numbers
- Plays games such as Simon Says

CHECKLIST OF EXPECTED THINKING SKILLS

Birth to fifteen months
- Reaches and grasps objects intentionally
- Recognizes objects and people
- Is aware of basic body parts
- Uses all five senses to gain information
- Is aware that certain events follow other events (crying brings parents)
- Performs an action to see the effect (drops object on the floor for someone to pick up)
- Imitates play of others

By two-and-a-half years
- Learns and expects routine
- Sees similarities and differences in objects and people

- Groups similar objects on the basis of one characteristic
- Relies on senses to gain information
- Shows some control of the environment (turns off faucets, shuts off lights)
- Understands that events can be sequenced
- Recalls recent events
- Expects absent people or objects to reappear at appropriate time or place
- Begins to solve problems and make decisions

By five years

- Recognizes similarities and differences in shapes, patterns, and figures
- Copies simple shapes (square, circle, triangle)
- Identifies missing parts in pictures
- Maintains attention on adult-directed tasks for short periods of time
- Maintains attention on own tasks for longer periods of time
- Practices to gain mastery of tasks
- Gets information by observing and asking questions
- Begins to link past and present information
- Begins to develop simple memory strategies
- Begins to recognize differences between the real world and fantasy
- Realizes actions have both a cause and effect
- Makes simple generalizations
- Groups objects on the basis of one or more characteristics
- Tells what happened first, second, and third
- Shows understanding of general times of day (morning, noon, night)
- Knows colors

CHECKLIST OF EXPECTED FINE MOTOR SKILLS

Birth to fifteen months

- Uses reaching and holding reflexes
- Puts objects in hands and mouth
- Picks up objects with a palm grasp
- Grasps and releases an object

- Handles objects with either hand
- Transfers object from one hand to the other
- Likes manipulating small objects
- Uses spoon as tool to bring food to his/her mouth
- Uses one finger to poke or push an object
- Tears paper
- Stacks blocks
- Uses thumb and forefinger
- Crams many objects into hands
- Turns pages in a book

By two-and-a-half years
- Uses a palm grasp when scribbling
- Uses thumb and forefinger to grasp an object
- Drinks out of a sipper cup
- Throws a large ball
- Shows a hand preference
- Uses a marker on paper
- Uses a pegboard
- Strings beads
- Squeezes a toy
- Turns knobs
- Works Velcro
- Handles snaps
- Screws on tops

By five years
- Manipulates small objects with both hands
- Builds with building toys
- Kneads dough
- Cuts with scissors
- Holds crayons appropriately
- Colors a picture
- Draws a person with at least six body parts
- Traces, copies, and draws basic shapes
- Folds triangles from squares
- Copies a design

- Copies a letter
- Pastes objects on a piece of paper
- Cuts out simple shapes
- Writes numerals 1 to 15
- Uses a fork correctly
- Laces shoes
- Ties knots
- Buttons a coat
- Paints a picture
- Pounds in pegs with control
- Picks up and fits objects together with ease
- Pours liquid into a glass without spilling
- Puts a ten-piece puzzle together
- Makes shadow shapes on the wall
- Spreads peanut butter on a piece of bread

CHECKLIST OF EXPECTED SOCIAL SKILLS

Birth to fifteen months
- Waves bye-bye
- Imitates behavior of parents and caretakers
- Responds to or imitates games such as Pat-a-Cake
- Anticipates feeding, dressing, and bathing
- Distinguishes between familiar people and strangers
- Adapts to changing people and places
- Shows considerable interest in peers
- Enjoys exploring objects with another person
- Gets others to do things for his/her pleasure
- Gives and takes objects

By two-and-a-half years
- Imitates behavior of peers and adults
- Plays alongside another child
- Calls some children friends
- Enjoys small-group activities for short periods of time
- Starts to see benefits of cooperation

- Has some awareness of the feelings of others
- Shows some control of impulses in dealing with others
- Starts to recognize that others have rights and privileges
- Begins to assert self appropriately in some situations

By five years
- Approaches new people with interest
- Begins to show awareness of similarities and differences among people
- Begins to have empathy for others
- Begins to function as a group member
- Uses play to explore social roles
- Manages peer conflict constructively
- Begins to share with others
- Starts to take turns
- Functions as a leader or follower in play situations
- Does not interfere with the work of others
- Asserts rights appropriately
- Begins to follow rules
- Recognizes authority
- Makes appropriate social responses
- Seeks help when needed

CHECKLIST OF EXPECTED SELF-HELP SKILLS

Birth to fifteen months
- Has developed senses
- Looks at a body part when it is touched
- Places objects in hands
- Clasps hands and fingers together
- Begins to use a spoon

By two-and-a-half years
- Attempts to go to the bathroom without help
- Washes hands
- Combs hair
- Brushes teeth
- Puts on socks

- Puts on shoes
- Feeds self

By five years
- Completes toilet skills
- Dresses and undresses self completely
- Washes face and hands
- Knows how to use a handkerchief or tissue
- Fastens buckles
- Buttons shirts, pants, and coats
- Zips zippers
- Opens and closes snaps
- Puts on boots
- Puts on gloves or mittens
- Uses a spoon or fork effectively
- Uses a knife for spreading
- Pours a drink
- Takes toys out to play with them
- Puts toys away

CHECKLIST OF EXPECTED SELF-ESTEEM SKILLS

Birth to fifteen months
- Shows intense feelings for parents
- Shows affection for familiar person through hugs and smiles
- Shows pride and pleasure in mastering tasks
- Expresses clearly differentiated emotions such as pleasure, disappointment, anger, fear, joy, and excitement
- Puts self to sleep
- Begins to quiet self
- Asserts self

By two-and-a-half years
- Differentiates facial expressions of anger, sadness, and joy
- Demonstrates awareness of own feelings
- Demonstrates awareness of others' feelings
- Expresses feelings through dramatic play

- Verbalizes feelings
- Shows increased control of emotions
- Begins to sense what is acceptable and unacceptable behavior
- Shows pride in new accomplishments
- Begins to appreciate own competency
- Has emerging sense of self

By five years

- Begins to recognize and label emotions such as anger, happiness, sadness, and fear
- Expresses both positive and negative feelings
- Has knowledge of own gender and ethnic background
- Has initiative to try new things
- Acts confident in new situations
- Makes decisions
- Postpones gratification
- Begins to exercise self-control
- Is not easily frustrated
- Does not cry easily
- Displays even temper
- Understands the idea of acceptable behavior
- Does not require constant support from parents or caregivers
- Separates from parents without being upset
- Starts to understand own strengths and limitations
- Has strong and positive sense of self

CHECKLIST OF EXPECTED SPEAKING SKILLS

Birth to fifteen months

- Coos and gurgles in infancy
- Repeats same sounds frequently
- Cries differently for different needs
- Babbles, using different sounds
- Uses voice to get attention
- Uses voice to establish social contact
- Enjoys imitating sounds
- Enjoys making sounds of familiar animals and objects

- Laughs a lot
- Says a few words such as "mama" and "dada"

By two-and-a-half years

- Uses more words than gestures
- Asks questions
- Responds to simple questions
- Repeats requests
- Names pictures
- Forms some plurals
- Uses two- and three-word sentences ("Eat cookie")
- Carries on conversation with self and dolls
- Refers to self by name
- Begins to verbalize some feelings
- Participates in conversations

By five years

- Produces understandable speech
- Labels familiar objects, people, and actions
- Defines objects by use (you drink from a glass)
- Uses descriptive words (large, good, cute)
- Uses the same sentence structure as family members
- Speaks in complete sentences
- Uses sentences of five to six words
- Asks questions for information
- Gives commands
- Varies intensity and tone of voice appropriately
- Sings simple songs
- Tells about recent personal experiences accurately
- Tells familiar stories
- Makes up pretend stories

CHECKLIST OF EXPECTED PREREADING SKILLS

Birth to fifteen months

- Enjoys hearing stories, poems, and rhymes
- Enjoys looking at picture books

By two-and-a-half years

- Shows preference for certain books
- Enjoys hearing stories, poems, and rhymes
- Retells stories
- Has the beginnings of a personal library

By five years

- Expresses self verbally
- Tells stories
- Looks at pictures and tells stories
- Repeats a sentence of six to eight words
- Answers questions about a short story
- Completes an incomplete sentence with the proper word
- Looks at books and magazines
- Enjoys hearing stories, poems, and rhymes
- Identifies rhyming words
- Knows some beginning sounds
- Makes fine visual discriminations
- Knows what an alphabet letter is
- Identifies some alphabet letters
- Recognizes some common sight words such as *stop*
- Pretends to read
- Understands that print carries a message
- Understands the conventions of print
- Has a personal library

CHECKLIST OF EXPECTED MATH SKILLS

Birth to fifteen months

- Judges the distance of an object from self correctly
- Uses all five senses to explore objects
- Identifies an object from different viewpoints
- Sees similarities in some objects
- Is aware that certain events regularly occur after others

By two-and-a-half years

- Uses senses to gain information about objects
- Describes properties of objects (color, shape)

- Sees similarities and differences in objects
- Compares objects by size (big, little)
- Understands objects can be put in order (big, bigger)
- Understands events can be sequenced
- Begins to count objects in sequence (one ball, two balls)

By five years

- Recognizes likenesses and differences in shapes
- Sorts similar objects by color, size, and shape
- Matches objects based on shape
- Recognizes circles, squares, and triangles
- Copies simple shapes (circle, square, triangle)
- Understands concept of longest and shortest
- Understands concept of more and less
- Knows position words such as *on, behind, under*
- Counts objects in sequence to five (one ball, two balls)
- Recognizes groups of one to five objects
- Counts to five
- Arranges blocks in order by size

CHECKLIST OF EXPECTED GROSS MOTOR SKILLS

Birth to fifteen months

- Lifts head
- Holds head up
- Sits without help
- Rolls over
- Crawls
- Crawls up stairs
- Crawls down stairs backward
- Pulls up to a standing position
- Balances on two feet
- Stands alone
- Takes a step
- Walks
- Walks and pushes an object

- Walks and carries a toy
- Throws an object

By two-and-a-half years

- Walks on uneven surfaces
- Walks backward
- Walks up stairs using both feet and relying on support
- Climbs
- Starts to run
- Jumps off one step
- Rides small toy by pushing with feet
- Sits alone in a small chair
- Catches a ball
- Rolls a ball
- Pulls an object
- Copies simple movements

By five years

- Bends
- Walks a straight line
- Walks sideways
- Walks up and down stairs alternating feet
- Stands on tiptoes
- Walks on tiptoes
- Walks on low balance beam
- Marches
- Runs
- Jumps forward
- Jumps continuously
- Jumps backward
- Jumps and lands on both feet in one spot
- Jumps rope
- Skips
- Gallops
- Leaps
- Hops
- Stands on one foot with eyes open for five seconds

- Stands on one foot with eyes closed
- Drops and catches a ball
- Bounces a ball
- Kicks a ball
- Swings
- Pedals a tricycle or bicycle

HOW CAREGIVERS LEARN ABOUT CHILDREN AND THEIR DEVELOPMENT

Caregivers can learn about children and especially about how they develop through taking formal classes. This includes classes offered by the Council for Early Childhood Professional Recognition and Child Care Resource and Referral Agencies in the United States and those given by the Canadian Child Care Federation. In both countries, nanny training programs, the Red Cross, continuing education programs, and campus and online college courses also present this important information.

In addition, there are many books that help caregivers learn more about the development and care of children. Here is a list of a few of these books:

Eisenberg, Arlene, Heidi Murkoff, and Sandee Hathaway. *What to Expect the First Year*, Second Edition. New York: Prentice Hall, 2003.

Feldman, Robert S. *Child Development,* Fourth Edition. Upper Saddle River, NJ: Workman Publishing Company, 2006.

Mayes, Linda C., and Donald J. Cohen. *The Yale Child Study Center Guide to Understanding Your Child: Healthy Development from Birth to Adolescence.* Boston: Little Brown and Company, 2003.

CHAPTER 5

WORKING IN CHILD CARE CENTERS

Young children receive a wide range of care, from the personal care of their parents to being cared for in a child care center. These centers go by different names. They can also be called daycare centers or nursery schools. They typically provide daytime training, supervision, and recreation for young children from just a few months old until they enter kindergarten. In both the United States and Canada, the regulation of the operation of child care centers is left to the states and provinces, respectively. Therefore, centers in Missouri may not be following the same rules as those in Oregon, nor will centers in Manitoba necessarily follow the same rules as those in Ontario. All of these centers, however, present the opportunity to work with others in providing child care to young children.

CHILD CARE WORKERS ARE NEEDED

About 50 million women of the close to 120 million women age sixteen years and older in the workforce in the United States today are working mothers. The U.S. labor force has experienced a revolution with the entry of working mothers in dramatic numbers. As recently as 1975, only one-third of women with children worked outside the home. Now, approximately 70 percent of all mothers work in this country. It's a similar story in Canada, where about 66 percent of all women with children under the age of three work, and about 75 percent of those whose youngest child is age three to five work. The major impact of this change in the workforce is the overwhelming demand that now exists for child care workers.

As the children of working mothers move through school, there will be a need for more child care workers for supervision of before- and after-school activities and during vacations and holidays from school. More workers are also needed because of the very high turnover rate among child care workers. Approximately one-third of all child care workers leave this profession each year. The National Women's Law Center attributes this to the fact that child care workers are among the lowest-paid workers in the United States, with wages only slightly above the poverty threshold. This is also true in Canada, where many workers earn local minimum wages. These very important caregivers in both countries actually earn less than many pet sitters.

MANY CHOICES FOR WORKING WITH CHILDREN

As the number of working mothers has increased, a need for a variety of child care arrangements has emerged. This, of course, has created many career choices that center on the care of children. Although approximately 20 percent of all families in the United States and 40 percent in Canada rely on relatives for satisfactory child care arrangements, the rest must look for help beyond their immediate family circle. The two most popular choices are child care centers and family child care homes. This chapter explores the different types of child care centers and the job opportunities they offer. Careers in family child care homes will be investigated in Chapter 4.

HISTORY OF CHILD CARE CENTERS

Before the Industrial Revolution, children were typically cared for in their homes by their families or by caregivers hired to assist family members. In the mid-1700s, factories sprouted up all over England and Scotland, and large numbers of women left their homes to work in them. This change was due largely to the invention of two machines, the spinning jenny and the water frame, which took the manufacture of textiles out of homes and into factories. Women were not able to leave their young children at home nor have the children at their sides in the factories while they were working. To solve this problem, factory owners established rooms for their workers' children and hired untrained adults, boys, and girls to supervise the children. These were the first child care centers. The establishment of child care centers in the United States occurred almost a hundred years later, when manufacturing became a major industry and women first joined the workforce.

Besides pioneering child care centers, Great Britain also introduced nursery schools a short time later to improve upon the care children were receiving at factory child care facilities. Robert Owen, a mill owner and social reformer, set up the first program to teach and supervise the children of factory workers and hired people with some teaching qualifications.

During World War II, women were needed to work in the factories. The U.S. government responded by passing the Lanham Act, which provided funds to set up child care centers in defense plants. At the end of the war, these centers were shut down, and many women left the workforce. In the 1960s, 1970s, and 1980s, women began returning to the workforce and the need for child care centers grew. Today, there are more than a hundred thousand centers serving young children.

In the mid-1960s, the federal government began to play a more prominent role in the care and development of young children. The Head Start program was launched to help prepare the children of poor families for school. Activities were designed to stimulate the social, emotional, mental, and physical growth of young children. Many parents of children in this program work in centers as aides or as volunteers. The Head Start program continues today. Also, the federal government began to provide some child care services for mothers receiving welfare payments who were enrolled in job training programs.

Many proposals for federally sponsored child care programs have been introduced since the 1960s in the United States and Canada. A comprehensive proposal, the Child Development Act, was passed in the U.S. Congress in 1971 but was vetoed by President Nixon. This legislation would have expanded Head Start and provided preschool education for all children who needed this help before enrolling in school. Every year child care bills are introduced in Congress; however, no comprehensive national child care plan has yet emerged. Some states have begun to offer prekindergarten programs for four-year-olds in their most disadvantaged school districts. And others are considering legislation requiring all schools to offer programs for three- and four-year-olds. A wide variety of child care programs are subsidized by federal, state, and local governments, and more will appear in the future to meet the demand for quality child care. Canada now has a Universal Child Care Benefit that will give parents C$1,200 a year per child under age six but, for the present, has rejected a plan to create much-needed, licensed child care spaces.

During the 1980s, business and industry became aware that working mothers with young children had more absences from work and left their jobs more often owing to the responsibility of caring for their children. The problems were greatest with the mothers of preschool children. In response, employers devised child care options to help their working mothers. A few have developed both on-site and off-site child care centers. In some cases, a group of employers have joined together to provide child care for their employees. An employer may also establish a referral service to help families find child care. Many employers offer vouchers for child care or include some form of child care in their benefits packages. With research showing that employer-sponsored day care programs improve morale and cut personnel costs, more companies have started some type of child care program. This trend is expected to continue, and to accelerate, in the future.

OWNERSHIP OF CHILD CARE CENTERS

While all child care centers are organized to care for young children, there is diversity in the ownership of these centers. Most centers in the United States are operated by nonprofit organizations. In Canada, it is the same story, with 80 percent of the child care centers operated on a not-for-profit basis—usually by community-based or parent organizations. Although people hear a lot about national child care chains, most of the for-profit child care centers are locally owned. The ownership composition of child care centers in the United States is shown in Figure 3.1.

There are advantages in having so many different types of child care centers. Not only do parents have a choice, but child care workers also can choose the work environment that is most appealing to them.

Nonprofit Child Care Centers

Two-thirds of all child care centers in the United States are nonprofit centers. They are operated by religious organizations, YMCA groups, public

Figure 3.1: Ownership of Child Care Centers

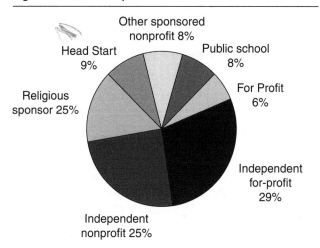

schools, parent associations, local organizations, recreation and park districts, and government services. These centers vary immensely in their size and the services offered. A center may have just one room with a teacher and an assistant teacher or several rooms and more than twenty staff members. It may be licensed for twenty children or more than a hundred. Nevertheless, nonprofit child care centers generate the greatest number of positions for child care workers.

Step One School. This school is an excellent example of a nonprofit child care center. The center is a nonprofit public benefit corporation governed by a board of directors. The staff consists of codirectors and nineteen teachers. Surprisingly, six of these teachers are men, an unusual occurrence in this career. All the teachers are salaried and are also paid overtime for meetings and conferences. The school has an innovative benefits program that lets staff apply benefits dollars to the specific benefit programs they want. And they also have a retirement program with matching benefits.

The school is easily accessible by public transportation. The building, formerly a K-3 public school, is situated on a prime site with views of San Francisco Bay. It contains five sunny and airy classrooms and a kitchen. The fenced yard provides a safe area for climbing, sand play, bike riding, and just sitting on the grass. A shrub-covered hill has trails for hiking and exploration and considerable space for gardening, especially organic gardening.

The goal at Step One is to guide the development of well-rounded children—children who know and trust themselves, who can get along with others, and who can recognize and follow their interests as well as create new ones. Both the indoor and outdoor environments are carefully designed by the staff to set the stage for play, which is the work of the child.

The children learn through experimenting, playing independently, building, and engaging in games and art projects they find attractive and interesting. Through their play and social interactions, the children discover more about the world they live in, build concepts, and learn to express their feelings in appropriate ways.

The school offers four programs: a program for two-year-olds, a nursery school program, a kindergarten program, and an afternoon program that extends care for children in the morning program. The teachers for each of the programs work together to develop an overall schedule of activities that meets the needs of the children. The curriculum is planned each week at classroom team meetings in which the events and progress of the last week are evaluated and new projects are developed collectively.

Step One has an open admissions policy that accepts children on a first-come, first-served basis, with adjustments for age and sex. The school is committed to having a diverse population of families and actively recruits in the community to achieve this. Step One also has an active scholarship program.

For-Profit Child Care Centers

Approximately 35 percent of all child care centers in the United States are for-profit. Most are independent rather than being part of a local or national chain. Teachers and assistant teachers usually receive hourly wages. The general rule regarding benefits is the smaller the center, the fewer the benefits.

Kid Time. Located in a suburban community, this school is a good example of a small, for-profit child care center. The school is principally owned by Stephen Wilson, who teaches at the center. As is typical of small centers, the director also teaches. All together, four full-time teachers and an assistant teacher care for approximately thirty-five to forty children each day. The director of Kid Time is salaried, while the teachers receive hourly wages. Some medical benefits are available for the staff. The center provides five sick/personal days, two weeks of vacation after one year of employment, and paid holidays.

The school is open all year except for eight major holidays. Hours are from 7:00 A.M. to 6:30 P.M., which are standard operating hours for many child care centers. Classes are offered for toddlers, preschoolers, and prekindergartners. More than half of the children stay all day. The morning program is basically preschool in nature, and some preschool work is also done in the afternoon.

Kid Time is located in an old home that has been expanded to accommodate the center. The atmosphere is intentionally very homelike to help the young children make a smooth transition between home and center. There is a large room for classes, another room for conducting group activities, and a kitchen, bathroom, and utility/art room.

For-Profit Child Care Chains

Only 6 percent of all child care centers in the United States are operated by chains. Some of these chains have extended their operation into Canada. In the United States, there are two giants: KinderCare, with over 1,200 centers, and La Petite Academy, with more than 700 academies. Other large for-profit centers are Knowledge Learning, providing services at some 300 centers and Bright Horizons Family Solutions with some 460 centers. These chains have standardized curriculums, policies, and operating rules. They offer considerably more amenities and services than the smaller child care centers, but their tuition is usually higher. For child care workers, employment with national chains usually means the opportunity to have some benefits, such as medical, dental, and life insurance, and a 401(k). Smaller neighborhood centers typically will not be able to offer these benefits.

In recent years, the chains have been expanding into new areas by opening centers in places close to parents' workplaces. The Bright Horizons Family Solutions chain provides corporate-sponsored worksite child care. In addition, centers that cater to children ages six and up have been started. They offer only before- and after-school care, including taking children to school and picking them up after.

Employer-Sponsored Child Care Centers

Although employers are definitely concerned with the issue of child care, few companies actually offer it on-site. An example of this type of facility is the Hacienda Child Development Center, located in its own building in a large industrial park housing several nationally known firms. The center has received international recognition for its innovative design, which features large windows and spacious outdoor play areas. Such amenities as a partially covered outdoor play area, air-conditioning, and radiant heating provide for the children's comfort and necessities, even in extreme weather.

The Hacienda Child Development Center. Here can be found the services that most working parents require. It is open from 7:30 A.M. to 6:00 P.M. five days a week and operates year-round on a business calendar. Employees working in the Hacienda Business Park receive a discount, as do employers who become corporate associates or corporate members of the Early Learning Institute (ELI), which operates the center. ELI operates its own centers as well as private centers under management contracts.

The professional staff receive a salary based upon their education and experience. Permanent, full-time staff receive health, dental, and vision insurance, retirement plans, flexible pretax spending accounts, child care subsidies, a credit union, paid holidays, seniority sabbaticals, sick and vacation days, and paid time off for program observations, jury duty, and bereavement. In all programs, the center exceeds the minimum staffing ratios required by state law. The infant program maintains a maximum 3 to 1 ratio rather than the required 4 to 1 ratio, while the toddler program maintains a maximum 4 to 1 ratio. The two-year-old and preschool programs maintain maximum 8 to 1 and 10 to 1 ratios, respectively, rather than the state 12 to 1 requirement.

The center offers care for infants, toddlers, preschoolers, and kindergartners. The infant and toddler programs are based on ELI's innovative HeadsUp! approach, which makes use of play and learning games to help lay the necessary foundations for future learning. The preschool program is a modified Montessori curriculum incorporating art, music, and imaginative play into the traditional emphasis on practical life, sensorial, language, mathematics, science, and cultural activities. The elementary program comprises a self-paced, individualized curriculum that continues and expands upon the Montessori curriculum employed in the preschool program.

The center makes a strong effort to keep parents involved. Parents receive written daily activity reports. They are also urged to attend the parent education meetings held once a month to keep parents informed on a wide variety of topics.

Extended-Day Child Care Centers for School-Age Children

The most rapidly developing area of child care is extended-day child care. This care is offered at hours when school is traditionally not in session and is designed for children who are enrolled in kindergarten through junior high or middle school. These programs are operated by a wide variety of institutions including schools, child care centers, home-based child care providers, recreation centers, and youth-serving organizations. Many programs offer van service to and from the schools the children are attending or are located within walking distance of the schools. Extended-day programs typically offer homework time, supervised care, and indoor and outdoor space for play. Some programs also offer enrichment, academic instruction, and special classes in areas such as dance, computers, music, and various sports.

The demand for more extended-day child care programs increases the need for child care workers. At child care centers that also care for younger children, existing personnel as well as part-time workers will provide the care. At centers that offer only before- and after-school care, personnel will work just during these sessions. This type of care is also very important in Canada, where children under the age of twelve cannot by law be left home alone.

REQUIRED SKILLS FOR CHILD CARE CENTER WORKERS

No one should ever consider a career working in a child care center unless the individual has a sincere desire to work with children. To be an effective worker, a knowledge of child development and child-rearing practices is also a prerequisite. In addition, certain aptitudes are key to working well with children. Child care workers need to have:

- Nurturing skills
- Sensitivity to the feelings of children

- Excellent communication skills with children
- An abundance of patience
- A tolerance of the clutter that surrounds young children
- A calm disposition

In doing this type of work, it is also essential to have good health, since child care workers are exposed to many illnesses while working with young children. Furthermore, it is helpful to have the physical stamina to bend and lift both children and materials throughout the day. Because children are so energetic, child care workers need to have a lot of energy. Skills in music, art, drama, and storytelling are important, too.

Child care workers work closely with other employees at a center. For example, three or four teachers and assistant teachers may be caring for thirty three-year-olds within one room. In this situation, considerable cooperation is required to handle the children. For this reason, child care workers need to be willing to be team players who listen to each other's suggestions and readily share ideas.

TRAINING IN THE UNITED STATES

In the past, it was possible to work at a child care center with no qualifications except an ability to work well with children, or even just an interest in working with children. While it still may be possible in a few states to find a job at a center with absolutely no training in early childhood education or development, most states now have legislation requiring child care workers to have taken certain courses or training in order to be hired. An ever increasing number of employers now require an associate's degree in early childhood education.

Child Development Associate Credential

Many states require child care workers to have the Child Development Associate (CDA) credential offered by the Council for Early Childhood Professional Recognition. The CDA program consists of two parts: CDA training and CDA assessment. The training portion, which teaches skills needed by child care center workers and home-based child care providers, is offered in local schools and colleges. Completion of the training program is not required for assessment, but assessment is necessary to obtain the credential. The assessment is made by a team of child care professionals from the Council for Early Childhood Professional Recognition. It involves showing the team that the applicant has the required skills and knowledge about child care, whether acquired through formal training or experience. You can obtain more information about eligibility requirements and a description of the credential by contacting the Council for Early Childhood Professional Recognition, 2460 16th Street NW, Washington, DC 20009-3575, or visiting the organization's website at cdacouncil.org.

Certified Childcare Professional

Some employers prefer hiring child care workers who have earned nationally recognized certification, such as the CDA or the Certified Childcare Professional (CCP). The CCP is earned by teachers who want to demonstrate their knowledge of early childhood development and their skills in working with young children. Contact the National Child Care Association for more information at 2025 M Street, NW, Suite 800, Washington, DC 20036-3309, or online at nccanet.org.

Associate of Arts and Bachelor's Degrees in Early Childhood Education

The associate of arts (A.A.) in early childhood education is typically a sixty-semester-unit program at a community college. Individuals have to fulfill general degree requirements by taking classes in such subjects as English, mathematics, science, and history, plus classes in early childhood education. The advantage of an A.A. is that these classes can usually be transferred to a college or university and used toward getting a bachelor's degree. And of course, each additional degree only makes applicants more attractive as candidates for jobs in the child care field, and helps them start their careers further up on the career ladder as well.

Only a few child care centers require applicants to have a bachelor's degree in order to qualify for teaching positions. However, this degree does give its holders a chance to start at many centers as a head or lead teacher. It also is a prerequisite for many positions as assistant director or director.

Private Centers in California

California is one state that demands that child care workers have considerable course work in early childhood education in order to work in both private and public child care centers. More training is required to work at public centers. The following employment requirements state the training applicants must have in order to work in private child care centers. Additional classes in safety and health, such as CPR and first aid, may be needed to work at a center. Also, the requirements to work at a center for school-age children are slightly different.

Aide. Aides must be at least eighteen years of age, be high school graduates, and be under the supervision of a qualified teacher at all times.

Teacher. The state requires teachers in private centers, both profit and non-profit, to complete a minimum of twelve college-level units of early childhood education courses, with at least one course in each of the following areas:

- Child development/psychology (3 units)
- Child, family, and community (3 units)
- Curriculum (6 units)

Some private centers may hire as teachers individuals who have completed six units of early childhood education courses, provided they are currently enrolled in a further six units.

Director. Directors must have the twelve units of early childhood education required for teachers, three units in administration, and four years of experience in a licensed center. Individuals with an associate of arts degree (A.A.) in early childhood education need two years of experience in a licensed center plus three units in administration, and those with a bachelor of arts (B.A.) in early childhood education need a children's center supervisory permit or one year of administrative experience in a licensed center.

TRAINING IN CANADA

In Canada, each province has its own specifications for staff training in regulated child care centers. Some have their own credentialing system. According to the Childcare Research Unit of the University of Toronto, no province requires staff to have university-level training in early childhood education. Also, the length of training required for staff varies from none to a community college certificate or diploma of one to three years. Three of the provinces require all staff to have regular professional development, and five provinces require all staff to have a first-aid certificate. The center director in seven of the provinces needs to have early childhood education training of one or two years. And in one province, directors must have a one-year community college certificate or diploma of one to three years.

POSITIONS FOR CHILD CARE WORKERS

The job titles used to describe child care workers vary from center to center. There is no standardization. The number and type of positions found in any center largely depend on its size. At a large child care center, the career ladder would look like this:

director
assistant director
head teacher
lead teacher
teacher
assistant teacher

The duties of both assistant teachers and teachers at a center depend greatly on the age level of the students. Teachers of infants and toddlers must necessarily spend considerable time in supplying basic care to the children. Diapers must be changed, bottles must be given, noses must be blown, shoes must be tied, children must be held and hugged, and assistance must be provided at mealtimes. The younger the children are, the greater the amount of attention that must be directed to caring for them. At the same time, it is important for the teachers to create an atmosphere in which the children can have a variety of experiences so that they will develop socially, emotionally, physically, and mentally. As the children grow older, teachers are able to concentrate more on giving the children educational experiences and less on supplying basic care. When the children are school-age and in extended-day child care programs, their teachers supervise their care, help them with homework, and plan recreational activities.

Profile of an Assistant Teacher

The entry-level position at child care centers is assistant teacher. The title of aide is frequently used to describe the job, as is teacher assistant. This is the one position in child care centers that does not require any early childhood education courses in some states. The main duty of the assistant teacher is to help the teacher in the classroom so that the program runs smoothly. In many centers, however, the assistant teacher and the teacher or teachers with whom he or she works share the tasks equally or almost equally.

Jane Kocourek is an assistant teacher of one-year-olds at one of the child care centers of a national chain. She is beginning at this level because she has not had the early childhood education courses required to be a teacher in her current home state, even though she has been a kindergarten teacher in another state. Jane and the other teacher share equally in the responsibilities of caring for eight young children. At all times a ratio of four children to one teacher must be maintained in keeping with state regulations on the number of children a teacher of one-year-olds may supervise. Each teacher does what is necessary at a given moment for the children in his or her room, following the general guidelines spelled out by the national chain for this age level. A typical schedule for Jane's day looks something like this:

8:00 A.M. On arrival, Jane usually sits on the floor playing with and talking to the children. She may even read stories to them. Diapers are changed as needed in the morning.

9:00 A.M. Snacks are served at a table. One teacher will clear the snack while the other remains with the young children. After the snack, the children go outside and play in the yard. Both teachers supervise this outside play session.

10:30 A.M. Lunch is served. The cook brings the meal to the room. While one teacher serves, the other sits with the children who require a little assistance to eat their lunch. After lunch, the children again play outside for approximately twenty minutes while both teachers watch them play.

11:30 A.M. The children lie down for their naps after all have had their diapers changed. The room is darkened, and the teachers use the first few minutes of naptime to wash the children's personal cups and bottles, remove garbage, and return luncheon dishes to the kitchen. When these tasks are completed, Jane goes to another area of the center and pulls out over sixty cots for the older children.

12:00 P.M. Jane enjoys a one-hour lunch break. As an hourly worker, she is not paid for this time.

1:00 P.M. Jane spends the next hour doing special tasks for the assistant director and director. One day she may trace letters for a bulletin board, while on another she may supervise a group that is napping.

2:00 P.M. The one-year-olds start waking up. Jane returns to the room and reads stories to some of the children as the others begin to wake up. She may also lead them in movement exercises to music. Then it is time to change all the children's diapers and serve the afternoon snack before going back outside again with the children.

3:30 P.M. The children return to their room and play with the blocks, manipulatives, and riding and pushing toys. Some may dress up, and others may play with the toy kitchen. Jane and the other teacher supervise their play and may suggest activities.

5:00 P.M. Parents begin to arrive to take the children home. Jane has to stay until the number of remaining children is four or fewer. Her workday officially ends at 5:00 P.M., so she receives overtime pay for additional time spent at the center.

Jane feels that she provides important nurturing to the children and helps them in learning verbalization skills. The children are getting a highly qualified assistant teacher who truly cares about them. When Jane obtains her California teaching credential, she plans to leave the child care center and to find a job teaching kindergarten.

Profile of a Teacher

Alice Bush works at a child care center that was designed for the parents who work in the business park where the center is located. She is an experienced teacher with a bachelor's degree in child development and has worked in Montessori child care centers. Alice has had considerable training in the Montessori approach, which is based on the philosophy of Maria Montessori, an Italian physician and educator who made remarkable progress with the education of slum children in Rome in the early part of the twentieth century. The cornerstone of the Montessori approach is a respect for the child as an individual striving for independence. The role of the Montessori teacher is to observe each child carefully and to facilitate learning through the child's own experiences. Alice utilizes her special training at the center, which follows a modified Montessori approach.

Alice works from 11:00 A.M. to 6:00 P.M. teaching thirty children between the ages of almost three through six. A head teacher, a lead teacher, and another teacher share the teaching responsibilities with her. The head teacher makes up the daily schedule, which is the same every day. The following describes Alice's day at work:

11:00 A.M. When Alice arrives, the children are outside in their play area. All of the teachers are supervising the children, making sure they are safe. None of the teachers are assigned to a specific group of children. Most of the time the children are engaged in free choice of activities; however, Alice or one of the other teachers may set up a game or a project, possibly doing something in the vegetable garden.

11:30 A.M. The children return inside for a group reading session. While one teacher reads to the children, the others are busy directing hand washing and bathroom activities, setting up for naptime, and organizing lunch. The teachers take turns handling these activities.

12:00 P.M. The children eat the lunches they have brought from home.

12:30 P.M. The older children leave to take part in the kindergarten program, which is held in another room. The rest of the children go down for naps. Alice stays with the nappers. While the children are resting, she is busy writing the daily reports that tell parents what their children have done that day. She also makes the afternoon snack and develops materials that will be used with the children.

3:00 P.M. The kindergarten children rejoin the group, and all enjoy a snack outside. Activities are low-key and similar to the earlier period outside. The head teacher goes in to do preparation work.

4:00 P.M. When the children return inside, the group becomes smaller as parents pick up their children. One of the teachers leaves. Alice may do preparation work or tell the children a story.

4:30 P.M. Alice will work with the children on an art project, direct a movement activity, or have the children play a musical game.

5:00 P.M. At 5:00 P.M. and 5:30 P.M., the other teachers leave, depending on the number of remaining children. Alice is then alone with the children, supervising them as they play with manipulatives, blocks, and other classroom materials. At the same time, she is checking the identification of parents and talking to them about their concerns.

Alice is committed to working with children. She fully believes the Montessori approach is the way to educate children for life. She plans to take more Montessori training to get her Montessori certificate.

What Being a Head Teacher Is Like

Within most child care centers, several teachers and assistant teachers work together in a classroom supervising the children and presenting educational activities. The teacher who is ultimately responsible for coordinating the efforts of all the teachers, taking care of the administrative work, and consulting with parents is called either a lead teacher or a head teacher, depending on the center. At some centers there is a head teacher as well as a lead teacher. In this case, the head teacher has the ultimate responsibility for the program, does the administrative work, and talks with the parents, while the lead teacher oversees what is happening in the classroom.

What Being an Assistant Director Is Like

The role of assistant director is not well defined. Quite often assistant directors are also part-time teachers. At some centers they will only handle administrative paperwork, while at others they may be in charge of the curriculum. Many child care centers, even large ones, do not have assistant directors. The one responsibility all assistant directors share is stepping in for the director whenever he or she is not at the center.

Suzanne Cox is the assistant director at one of the centers of a very large national chain of child care centers. Her only child care jobs have been at this center, where she started as a part-time assistant teacher with just three units of early childhood education. Suzanne swiftly advanced to teacher, as soon as she had sufficient early childhood education units, and then to assistant director, all within one year of starting at the center. She describes the position of assistant director as that of a director in training. Her duties and responsibilities at the center include:

- Handling the center's banking and bookkeeping
- Organizing all of the children's files
- Keeping track of immunization records
- Contacting substitute teachers
- Stepping in as a substitute teacher
- Administering medicine to children on medication
- Preparing accident reports
- Contacting parents of sick children
- Documenting and conducting fire drills
- Handling special projects such as writing a new curriculum for foreign students attending the center
- Driving a van run

Suzanne's duties are typical of assistant directors at centers associated with child care chains. She works from 8:00 A.M. to 5:00 P.M. She receives an hourly wage plus a benefits package that includes free child care for her daughter. Suzanne likes working for a national chain because it is easy to transfer to another center.

Profile of a Director

The director has the ultimate responsibility for all facets of the operation of a child care center. Depending on the ownership, he or she will justify the operation of a center to a board of directors (nonprofit), a divisional manager (chain), or an owner or group of owners (independent, for-profit). By studying the day of a director, it is possible to understand how many tasks directors must handle.

Being a director, according to Linda Owens, is akin to being an expert in crisis management, since the director is responsible for every aspect of running a child care center. This can mean coming to the school at 1:00 A.M. when the burglar alarm goes off, or finding yourself driving the early run of the center van because the van driver called in sick at the last minute. In addition, the director is the one who has 100 percent responsibility for the profit and loss of the center.

Linda is director of a child care center with a capacity of 160 children. Currently the enrollment is 130 children, and the center has twenty-two teachers and assistant teachers (aides). Because she works at a child care center that is part of a national chain, she is responsible for following the company's policies and daily procedures.

As director, Linda has an amazing number of duties and responsibilities, including the following:

- Following all state regulations for child care centers
- Making sure the chain's curriculum is being followed
- Handling parental and staff complaints
- Hiring and firing center staff
- Making sure that tuition is paid for all children
- Counseling children with behavior problems
- Marketing the center
- Conducting monthly staff meetings
- Acting as a substitute teacher when necessary
- Visiting with parents as children are left off and picked up
- Providing tours of the center to prospective clients
- Making sure that the kindergarten is following state guidelines
- Checking that field trips are properly staffed
- Ensuring that the building is maintained in a proper manner and is clean

Linda holds an A.A. in early childhood education and is currently working on her master's in human development and counseling. Before becoming a director at this center, Linda was a teacher, an assistant director, and a director at another center. She plans to continue in her present work because she enjoys helping families care for their young children.

Profile of a Founder of a Child Care Center

Sue Britson had a dream of founding a child care center that would reflect her philosophy. She firmly believed that children's development socially, emotionally, mentally, and physically begins at a very young age and wanted to influence their development and work with their ideas. Sue had a master's degree in early childhood education plus several years of teaching experience. This gave her a solid background in understanding how child care centers operate, which is something needed to successfully establish a center.

The first step in starting up a school, according to Sue, is to decide upon your philosophy and mission. Then, by researching what other centers exist in an area, you can determine the appropriate niche for a new center to fill.

Next, you must find a suitable location for the center. A center for young children should be located in a safe area that is easily accessible to families, preferably near public transportation. In addition, Sue points out that the location must be zoned or capable of being zoned for a child care center. In selecting a site, be sure to consider whether the building meets, or can easily be made to meet, local and state licensing regulations. Passing an inspection from the local fire marshal is part of the process of selecting the right building for a center. And, of course, you will need seed money to start up: at least two months of operating expenses in the bank would be a sufficient amount.

Sue and her partner found a site in June in a room in a community recreation area. In September, their center opened, and classes were full within a week. From the first day, their center was a success because parents were so pleased to find professional teachers (with education and training) operating a center that stressed a developmental approach. Within two years, the partners and codirectors of the center realized that they must expand in order to pay themselves a living wage. Besides teaching at the center, Sue had to work thirty hours a week as a waitress to survive.

After carefully doing their research again, they relocated to a former K-3 school that was sold at an auction. This site offered five classrooms, a fenced yard, and an office complex. When the center reopened, it had an expanded high-quality program taught by professionals, and the teaching staff began to receive benefits and better wages. (The school is described earlier in this chapter.)

LOOKING AT CHILD CARE CENTER WORKERS IN THE UNITED STATES AND CANADA

By Gender

Overwhelmingly, child care center workers are female in both the United States and Canada, including the administrative positions of assistant director and director. Furthermore, positions in upper management, such as regional and divisional directors of national chains, are predominantly filled by women.

By Age

The staff of child care centers is young. Their median age is thirty-eight in the United States, compared with forty-four for all workers. About 5 percent of these workers are below the age of twenty. In Canada, 45 percent of the workers are under thirty years of age. Table 3.1 shows the distribution of child care staff and all industries by age group in the United States.

Table 3.1 Percent Distribution of Employment, by Age Group, 2004

Age Group	Child Daycare Services	All Industries
16–19	4.9	4.2
20–24	12.8	9.9
25–34	24.7	21.8
35–44	23.3	24.8
45–54	20.6	23.3
55–64	10.3	12.4
65 and older	3.5	3.5
Total	100%	100%

Source: Bureau of Labor Statistics

By Education

The majority of the staff at child care centers, even assistant teachers, have had some formal course work in early childhood education or child development in both the United States and Canada. As to be expected, the higher workers rise on the child care center career ladder, the higher their level of education is.

By Location

Jobs at day care centers can be found everywhere across the country; however, they are less common in rural areas.

By Size

The more than one hundred thousand licensed day care centers vary in size from the self-employed person caring for a few children in a private home to the large corporate-sponsored center with a sizable staff. Nearly all centers have fewer than fifty child care workers. In fact, more than 80 percent of child care centers employ fewer than twenty workers.

By Hours

Because many child care centers are open for twelve or more hours a day, workers' hours will vary. One or more workers must stay until all children are picked up by their parents or guardians. Nearly three out of ten full-time employees in the industry work more than forty hours a week. There are also many opportunities for part-time work.

SALARY AND FRINGE BENEFITS

Child care center workers are underpaid. They receive low hourly pay especially when compared to others with comparable training. According to the National Women's Law Center, the average yearly earnings for child care center workers is slightly more than $18,000 per year. Administrators in child care centers have a median hourly wage of around $18 per hour. The lowest 10 percent receive a little more than $11 per hour while the highest 10 percent receive more than $33 per hour. In Canada, child care workers are receiving wages equivalent to the local minimum wage in some communities.

Child care workers are constantly exposed to illness at work, which poses a serious risk to their health. Most do not get paid sick leave; however, their health benefits are improving, especially for teachers. But for most child care workers benefits are minimal. Many centers do offer free or discounted child care to employees which adds to the appeal of this job. Some offer a full benefits package, including health insurance and paid vacations. But many provide no benefits at all. A few are willing to cover the cost of courses taken at community colleges or technical schools.

Worthy Wage Day

The low wages of child care workers are beginning to get the attention of the general public because of the actions of advocacy groups. One effort promoting action by child care workers and care providers to secure a living wage and decent working conditions for themselves is Worthy Wage Day. The first national Worthy Wage Day was April 9, 1992. This day was designed to call attention to the low pay that child care workers receive and also to teach child care workers that it is perfectly acceptable for them to speak up about their low wages. On this day, workers were urged to take time off from their jobs to march, rally, and wear buttons to make the public aware of their need for "worthy" wages. Since then, every May 1st is recognized as Worthy Wage Day—to highlight the importance of quality care for children and its relation to worthy wages for child care work. Activities will vary from community to community.

EMPLOYMENT OUTLOOK

Job opportunities for workers in child care centers are good because of the high replacement needs in this career area. Qualified individuals should have no trouble finding jobs. Overall, employment in child care centers is expected to increase as fast as the average for all occupations through 2014. This is a result of a growing population of children under five years of age and fewer children being cared for by parents and relatives. Plus, more workers will be needed in after-school programs catering to older children. Demand for workers in centers could decrease if states begin to fund universal preschool. In Canada, the demand for workers will further accelerate as the government provides funds to end the shortage of centers and build more centers—thus employing more workers.

Working at child care centers has become more appealing even with its low pay as the federal government is forgiving college loans for those who study and work in the field of early childhood education. Plus, the government is providing the states with Child Care and Development Block Grants so more young children whose families are below the poverty line can enroll in child care centers—thus increasing the number of children in child care. Also, some centers are already paying their staff a satisfactory wage. Finally, the attention being focused on low wages makes it more likely that child care workers' salaries in the future will reflect their vital contributions to families and society.

CHAPTER

CARING FOR CHILDREN IN YOUR HOME

One of the choices that parents have when seeking quality child care for their children is family child care homes. Demand is high for this option as it lets parents have their children cared for in a home environment with just a few children. Plus, the children will have just one caregiver instead of the several typical of child care centers, letting them establish a firm bond with the caregiver. This type of care is especially popular with families seeking care for children younger than age three. It is also popular with those looking for before- and after-school care for their school-age children, which adds to the demand for home-based care.

There are more than two hundred thousand licensed family child care homes in the United States. Of this number, more than a third of the homes are small, family child care homes, which are usually eight or fewer children. Plus, there may be as many as one hundred thousand small unlicensed homes caring for four or five children. In Canada, about half of all children between six months and five years are being cared for by someone other than their parents. Of this group 30 percent are being cared for at child care centers and another 30 percent at home-based child care centers.

REQUIRED SKILLS FOR AT-HOME CHILD CAREGIVERS

Providing child care in one's home may sound like the perfect stay-at-home job for women—even letting them be with their own children full time.

However, the daily care of several children is challenging. Emergency situations must be handled. A solid developmental program for the children needs to be created and followed. The children must be shown how to play together. Parents who consistently pick their children up late or fail to pay on time must be dealt with. Successful providers are professionals who offer a valuable service and are far more than nurturing individuals who love children. A family child care provider should possess the career aptitudes described in the Chapter 1 section "Finding the Right Child Care Career" plus these special ones:

- Ability to take responsibility for the total care of several children
- Ability to juggle several activities at one time
- Willingness to work long hours
- Toleration of the wear and tear on the caregiver's home
- Willingness to commit to caring for children in the caregiver's home for a year or more
- Ability to discipline in a positive manner
- Willingness to create a program that meets the individual needs of each child
- Willingness to share information about each child's progress with parents
- Ability to offer the children a safe environment
- Ability to select and keep competent help
- Ability to deal effectively with parental complaints
- Good bookkeeping skills
- Willingness to keep accurate records for each child
- Ability to handle business aspects of child care professionally

WHERE TO FIND HELP IN SETTING UP A FAMILY CHILD CARE HOME

Starting a new business can be a challenging undertaking. So it is wise to do some research first. It's also important that the start-up operator is truly committed to being an entrepreneur. Fortunately, there are agencies throughout the United States that offer services to prospective family child care providers. These Child Care Resource and Referral (CCR&R) Agencies give child care providers the training, technical assistance, and support to develop high-quality child care programs. At the same time, they also help parents make informed choices in selecting care.

The number of CCR&R agencies has grown steadily since the 1980s, matching the increasing need for child care. Most CCR&Rs are private, local organizations created by parents or child care advocates. Only a few CCR&Rs are state or public agencies. Funding is provided by a combination of monies from city, county, state, and federal governmental units, businesses, corporate foundations, United Way agencies, service organizations, charitable organizations, and individuals. Approximately half of the states possess statewide networks that offer training and technical assistance to local CCR&R agencies. Before deciding to start a family child care home, prospective care providers should always consult with their local agency. Information on the location of the nearest CCR&R agency can be obtained by contacting the National Association of Child Care Resource and Referral Agencies, 1319 F Street NW, Suite 810, Washington, DC 20004, or by visiting the organization's website at naccrra.org.

The Canadian Child Care Federation has some information similar to CCR&R agencies. It also has a classroom and online training program for those who are interested in becoming providers of family child care in both the regulated and unregulated sectors. For all the basics in starting a child care program in the home, from setting it up to managing it, individuals should visit the government website Canada Business at cbsc.org. This website provides the names and addresses of provincial service centers that can be visited in person for more personal help.

Profile of a CCR&R Agency Employee

Phyllis Graser was one of the thousands of CCR&R employees who offered services to parents and child care providers. She worked for a private, not-for-profit corporation that had three area offices and two satellite offices. The offices offer the following services:

Parent services

- Referrals
- Subsidized child care
- Parent education

Provider services
- Provider development
- Nutrition education
- Recruitment/training

Advocacy
- Seminars and conferences
- Speakers bureau
- Bimonthly newsletter

Employer services
- Feasibility study
- Needs surveys
- Tuition assistance management

Agencies as well as offices of an agency do vary in the breadth of services they offer. At her office, Phyllis was the only employee. Besides helping parents find quality child care, she provided assistance to family child care home providers in these areas:

Licensing. Phyllis held orientation meetings to introduce prospective caregivers to the licensing process, which in her state is lengthy. Individuals need step-by-step guidance to complete this process.

Start-up meeting. Phyllis conducted a monthly orientation meeting on the business aspects of starting a home child care business. Help was given with marketing, insurance, taxes, and record keeping.

Referral list. Phyllis called local child care providers once a month to update the agency's list of licensed child care providers. Also, she checked on the number of spaces available by age level at the family child care homes.

Provider development. Phyllis arranged classes in cardiopulmonary resuscitation (CPR) and advanced training workshops for home caregivers. She also worked with individual providers to help them offer quality child care.

Child care food program. Child care providers are reimbursed by the Department of Agriculture for a portion of the cost for nutritious meals served. Phyllis linked providers with nutrition and health experts within the agency who assisted with meal planning and the paperwork necessary to become part of the food program.

BASIC STEPS INVOLVED IN STARTING A FAMILY CHILD CARE HOME

No matter whether a family child care home is being set up in the United States or Canada, the same steps need to be followed to create a quality program. First of all, it is necessary to decide whether your facility will be independent or associated with an organization. Many organizations, including churches, charities, and businesses as well as state/provincial and local government units, will contract with individuals to care for children in their homes. Not only will they help caregivers set up a home facility, they will also provide the children and pay for each child. The organizations typically provide advice on operating a family child care home and may offer some benefits. The disadvantage to this arrangement is that the caregiver largely becomes an employee rather than the owner of an independent business.

Checking on Government Regulations

One area of rules and regulations that all new family child care providers will need to comply with is that of licenses, permits, and regulations. Each city or municipality has the authority to issue its own business licenses within its jurisdiction. In addition, zoning regulations should be investigated. It may be necessary to go through the permit process. This involves proving that there is sufficient on-site parking for the employer and any employees, enough play area for each child, no concentration of child care facilities in the neighborhood, and an adequate pickup area for parents. It is best to check out all possible regulations before establishing a family child care business.

Obtaining a License

Prospective caregivers must determine whether a state or provincial license is required to operate a family child care home. Some states and provinces have very stringent requirements, and others have practically no requirements at all. The nearest CCR&R agency in the United States or Canada Business service center can provide this information, as can the state or provincial department responsible for licensing homes for child care. Licensing requires caregivers to meet certain minimum standards for health, safety, and staffing. For example, family child care homes in California must meet the following standards:

- Fingerprint and tuberculosis clearance of all adults over age eighteen in the home
- Certain fire and safety standards for the house
- Prohibition of all physical and humiliating punishment
- The right of parents to visit the home at any time
- Guns and ammunition locked up
- No smoking while children on premises
- Small-home license: eight children, provided two of the children are of school age, or only four children if under age two
- Large-home license: fourteen children with no more than four under age two, and an aide present for seven or more children

Family child care providers do not need to be licensed in California if care is provided to the children of only one family. Parents, however, can require providers to get a physical examination and TB clearance, references, take CPR and first-aid classes, and offer a smoke-free environment.

Getting a license when one is not required can seem unnecessarily time-consuming. On the other hand, parents tend to prefer family child care homes that are licensed because it implies professionalism and means that minimum standards have been met.

Becoming an Accredited Caregiver

Caregivers in the United States who want to be recognized as professionals providing high-quality care seek accreditation from the National Association for Family Child Care (NAFCC). In Canada, there is no national program. Instead, the provinces have their own programs. Accreditation by the NAFCC scrutinizes the following areas: relationships, environment, developmental learning activities, safety and health, and professional and business practices. The process involves using a self-study workbook to assess the caregiver's own program, designing a professional development plan to prepare for an observation visit, and making quality programs.

In order to be eligible for NAFCC accreditation, a caregiver must meet the following eligibility requirements:

- Be at least twenty-one years old
- Have a high school diploma or GED
- Provide care to children for a minimum of fifteen hours per week
- Provide care to a minimum of three children in a home environment. At least one child must live outside the provider's home.
- Be the primary caregiver, spending at least 80 percent of the operating hours actively involved with the children
- Have at least eighteen months experience as a family child care provider before the observation visit, or twelve months experience if home visits are conducted monthly and intensive training is received
- Meet the highest level of regulation to operate a family child care program
- Be in compliance with all regulations of the authorized licensing body

Participating in the Child Care Food Program

Family child care providers in the United States should investigate the Child and Adult Care Food Program (CACFP). The program, which is sponsored by the U.S. Department of Agriculture (USDA), reimburses child care providers for a portion of the cost for meals served. Its purpose is to improve the diets of children by offering well-balanced, nutritious meals and to help providers serve high-quality meals without passing the cost on to working parents. The program is administered locally through sponsors. CCR&R agencies sponsor the food program in many areas or know the name of the area sponsor. Furthermore, many sponsors will help with the program's paperwork, have menu suggestions, and provide nutrition education. Each month the home caregiver has to complete forms showing the number of meals and snacks served and menu forms. The meals must meet USDA requirements. It is necessary to reapply for admission to the program annually. There is no equivalent program in Canada.

SOUND BUSINESS PRACTICES NEED TO BE FOLLOWED

Successful family child care providers are good business people. Getting insurance, filing and paying taxes, keeping good records, setting fees, and writing contracts will play an important role in the operation of a quality child care home. Most CCR&R agencies and local Canada Business service centers will provide expert help in these areas. For example, some CCR&R agencies have books with forms that can be used for keeping records, bookkeeping, and contracts. Moreover, through agency education programs and newsletters, family child care providers can keep abreast of any changes in laws that may affect them.

Getting Insurance

One day Johnny hits Susie and stitches are required, or a parent trips and falls walking up the drive of the caregiver's home. Accidents happen, and child care providers need the protection of insurance from their first day of operation. Caregivers should be aware that homeowner's policies do not normally cover the operation of an in-home business. And unfortunately, the rates of insurance for child care providers have risen dramatically in recent years. The homeowner's insurance agent can give solid advice about insurance coverage and possibly place a rider on the existing policy to cover claims related to the child care business. Caregivers should also find out if insurance can be purchased through a local child care association.

Filing and Paying Taxes

Family child care providers need to pay federal and state or provincial taxes. It is also necessary to pay social security taxes for the caregiver and any employees. CCR&R agencies may have helpful materials or workshops devoted to the handling of taxes. In addition, the *Tax Guide for Small Business*, available from the Internal Revenue Service, is loaded with helpful information on filling out forms and on keeping books and records. In Canada, family child care providers need to study the Canada Revenue Agency's easy-to-understand guide *Using Your Home for Day Care*. It explains what expenses can be claimed, the employer's responsibilities, and the importance of keeping good records.

Keeping Good Records

If family child care providers don't keep good records, they will never know whether they are making a profit. Records are also needed to support all items of income and expense reported on tax returns. A bookkeeping system should be chosen before the business opens. It is helpful to have a separate bank account for business income and expenses. A petty cash fund should be established for small expenses. The invoice, paid receipt, or canceled check should be saved for every expense in a safe, well-organized file. Although most caregivers remember to keep a record of expenses for food, toys, helpers, and supplies, they may forget such items as professional magazines, organization dues, a percentage of the house utility bills, and fees for insurance premiums.

Setting Fees

To some degree, fees are determined by what other family child care providers within an area are charging. Study the marketplace to find out what other caregivers are charging, and then set a fee that will cover your expenses and produce a certain income. The local CCR&R agency should have information on low, middle, and high fees within the community. Where a caregiver lives can affect the fees he or she is able to charge. A 2006 survey by the National Association of Child Care Resource and Referral Agencies (NACCRRA) showed that in urban areas, providers charged $121 per week on average, in suburban areas, $117, and in rural areas, $97. In setting fees, it is essential to consider the following factors:

- The basic fee and how many hours are included
- Charges for additional time
- Charges for late pickup
- Meals and snacks to be included in fees
- The rate structure for different ages
- Charges for absences
- Discounts for siblings
- Charges for supplies (diapers, crayons)
- Charges for holidays

Once fees are set, create a policy sheet listing the fees and exactly how and when they are to be paid.

Writing a Contract

Contracts eliminate misunderstandings. They should spell out the rules under which the family child care home will operate. Parents need to know if care will be available on holidays, how arrivals and departures will be handled, and whether the children can bring toys from home. The contract should also include the fee schedule. Figure 4.1 consists of a sample contract from a CCR&R agency that caregivers can adapt to meet their needs.

Figure 4.1: Sample Family Child Care Contract

CONTRACT

Date _____

I agree to enroll my child _____ age _____
in the _____ Family Child Care Home,
beginning on _____. I have received and read the Family Child
Care Home Rules and agree to comply with all rules and responsibilities
as stated. This contract will be valid beginning _____. Two weeks
notice by either party will be required in order to terminate this contract.
This contract will be revised on an annual basis. Care will normally begin
at _____ o'clock and end at _____ o'clock on the following days of the
week: _____

Care will/will not include the following meals and snacks: _____.

The charge for care of the child is $_____ per _____.
Overtime charges are $_____ per _____.

Parents are expected to pay full rates for holidays, absences, and parent
vacations. Additional charges will be accrued for special dietary requests
or damages to the contractor's property.

Payment to the Family Child Care Provider will be made in advance.

Parents are to provide the names of any persons authorized to pick up children,
medical and insurance information, and any special dietary or health concerns.

(Optional) Payment obligation is based on the hours parents contract to use
child care.

_____
Provider Signature

_____   _____
Parent Signature   Address/Phone

_____   _____
Parent Signature   Address/Phone

_____
Date

Source: Contra Costa Child Care Council

Few family homes are set up to handle a family child care business. Physical changes may have to be made to the caregiver's home to provide an appropriate environment for children. Space will be needed for eating, sleeping, and playing. Many caregivers have to remodel part of their homes to acquire sufficient space. Frequently, garages are turned into interior play space. In addition, the outside play area will need to be fenced. All areas that the children will use must be made safe. This includes locking up or storing out of the children's reach all hazardous materials, knives, medicines, and matches; covering electrical outlets with safety caps; and locking up any guns or ammunition. A cubbyhole or bin should be provided for each child to use for storing extra clothing and take-home items.

The exact tools of the trade needed to launch a family child care home depend on the ages of the children for whom care will be offered. Caregivers will probably need most of the following items:

- Cribs, cots, or sleeping mats
- Television set and videocassette recorder (VCR)
- CD player and CDs
- Books, puzzles, and games
- Blocks and balls
- Manipulative toys such as Legos, small figures, and Tinkertoys
- Assorted toys from trucks to trains
- Art and craft materials
- Child-size tables and chairs
- Dress-up clothes
- Play kitchen and/or playhouse
- Dolls and stuffed animals
- Sandbox and sandbox toys
- First-aid kit
- Emergency supply of diapers and baby food

Not all of the materials will have to be purchased. Caregivers may already own many of the items. Friends may contribute toys and furniture to the caregiver, and some items can be borrowed from CCR&R agencies.

FAMILY CHILD CARE PROGRAMS NEED TO BE EDUCATIONALLY SOUND

The most important aspect of establishing any family child care home business is developing a program that is appropriate for the children. It needs to be designed to meet their developmental needs. Caregivers need to realize that young children learn through play. Having an adequate supply of playthings is essential so that the children can experiment, build, play games, and enjoy art activities alone and with others. The children's time should be divided between free choice of activities and group activities such as stories, music, and movement. Every day should have the same general schedule that can be adjusted to meet the children's needs. Before a family child care home opens for business, a daily schedule of activities should have been well thought out.

Child care providers who do not have a background in early childhood education should make use of the informational programs and materials offered by CCR&R agencies or the Canadian Child Care Federation as well as child care associations. They also should take courses in child care and child development, which are readily available at community colleges.

MARKETING THE FAMILY CHILD CARE BUSINESS

Once the home is prepared and the program is devised, the caregiver needs to market his or her service to families within the community who are looking for child care. Local CCR&R agencies can serve as advertisers in the United States. They provide parents seeking child care with the names of licensed caregivers, and they regularly update the number of current openings available by age group.

To attract business, caregivers need to market their service in a variety of ways in order to gain exposure to the widest possible number of prospective clients. Some suggestions on how to market a family child care business follow.

- **Word-of-mouth.** Tell everyone about the business; someone is certain to need child care services. It may turn out to be a friend of a friend or an acquaintance of the supermarket clerk.

- **Flyers.** Colorful flyers that attract attention should be placed in spots where working parents are likely to see them, such as on bulletin boards at grocery stores, churches, and YMCA/YWCAs.
- **Newspaper ads.** Placing ads in local newspapers, including shoppers, is another way to reach potential clients. Ads should specify the age groups for which care is offered, the hours of care provided, the special competencies of the caregiver, and the general location of the home.
- **The Internet.** Placing ads or information about your family child care business on local websites can be helpful. It is also a good idea to develop a website so online types can easily learn about your business.
- **Newsletters.** Companies, organizations, and churches often publish newsletters that have advertisements or occasionally write about services family child care homes offer.

Profile of a New Family Child Care Home Provider

Maureen B. Chahin has just started Kid Kelly Play and Learn, a family child care home. She is now caring for five children between the ages of eighteen months and three-and-a-half years in her home. One of the children is her own daughter. Maureen brings to her new business a solid background in early childhood education, having taught preschool, kindergarten, and elementary school in the past. She launched this business because she wanted to be near her daughter and liked working with children. With the help of her husband, she has approached starting her new business very professionally. By looking at the steps Maureen followed, we can see the actual effort required to start a family child care home business.

Step 1. Maureen attended the orientation class for prospective family child care home providers at the nearest CCR&R agency. She also purchased the agency's book, which contained sample forms and information on how to start up a family child care home.

Step 2. The licensing process for a large-home license (twelve children) was initiated. Maureen and her husband took TB tests and were fingerprinted. The backlog was so great that it took ninety-two days to get fingerprint clearance. The fire marshal visited three times before being satisfied that the home had met fire safety standards. More fire extinguishers and smoke detectors had to be installed. The major problem was finding a fire alarm that could be heard throughout the neighborhood.

Step 3. Maureen and her husband attended a business class at the CCR&R agency.

Step 4. Maureen obtained a business license from the city and checked to see that there were no zoning problems.

Step 5. Maureen's husband contacted their insurance agent over the phone and arranged accident and liability insurance.

Step 6. A bookkeeping system was established, as well as a file for storing receipts and pertinent business information.

Step 7. Maureen assessed the suitability of her home. The family trilevel home was perfect for caring for the children: the entire lower level could be used for the children. The family room became the children's playroom, and the bedroom was set up with cribs and cots for napping. There was also a bathroom and a door to the yard on this level. Gates had to be installed to keep the children from leaving the lower level as well as entering the upper level. One advantage of the trilevel home was that Maureen could prepare meals and snacks in the kitchen and see what the children were doing in the play area because of the openness of the house design.

Step 8. The yard was landscaped to provide a safe play area for the children. Soft bark was placed under the swing set, a sandbox was built, and a water table was installed.

Step 9. Maureen purchased sturdy toys, books, records, puzzles, a play kitchen, a push train set, and blocks to create a playroom full of exciting possibilities for the children to explore.

Step 10. Maureen decided on her policies and made up a parent handbook that covered her philosophy, the admissions policy, a statement of the rights of the licensing agency, and policies on arrival, departure, late pickup, and absence. The handbook also detailed her health and nutrition policies and how accidents and medication would be handled. Information was provided on clothing, napping and rest time, the children's cubbies, artwork, birthdays, field trips, toys from home, and discipline. A thorough explanation was given of the program, tuition payment policies, and the use of a parent's bulletin board to enhance parent/caregiver communication.

Step 11. Maureen engaged her sister as her helper and investigated the possibility of getting a high school student in the early childhood training program as a helper later on.

Step 12. Maureen began marketing her family child care home. She placed a notice in the neighborhood home-owner's newsletter and received five or six inquiries from this source. Word-of-mouth brought more prospective clients from a friend who ran a child care facility that was full. She ran an ad in the local newspaper and put flyers up at the local park and neighborhood stores. Her informative flyer is shown in Figure 4.2.

Step 13. Maureen received many phone calls about her child care business and began to show the home to interested parents. Almost everyone who saw the quality setup decided to enroll their children in her program.

Step 14. A daily schedule of activities was formulated for the children.

Step 15. The family child care home opened for business, and an information folder was created for each child.

Step 16. Steps were taken to enroll the home in the Child and Adult Care Food Program to get reimbursement for meals and snacks.

Profile of an Experienced Family Child Care Home Provider

Norma Manning has been caring for children in her home for more than fifteen years. She has stayed with this career so long because she truly enjoys being around children. Norma wants her home to operate like a warm family group. Norma belongs to an association of caregivers that meets monthly. She finds these meetings helpful because the caregivers share ideas, and there is always a speaker on a subject that interests her. For example, she may learn more about preparing healthy snacks, dealing with difficult children, or following the latest regulations.

Kid Kelly

Play and Learn

Tender Loving Child Care
in our Shadow Creek home.
California credentialed Teacher
with 7 years preschool, day care,
elementary school experience
enjoys working with Children!!!
Lots of fun activities daily.

Big backyard with

Sandbox, Swings, Castle & Water Table

Openings Available

18 months and up

Please Call Maureen
at 555-4052 to
make an appointment
to come by !!!!!!!

Norma's daily schedule is flexible. Some days she takes the children to the park or on a shopping expedition. She typically cares for six to eight children of diverse ages with the full-time help of a former kindergarten teacher. The daily schedule at Norma's home usually follows this pattern:

7:00 A.M.–9:00 A.M. The children arrive and are given breakfast, if needed.

9:00 A.M.–10:00 A.M. The children play alone or in groups with the variety of toys and games in the playroom. Some will watch television or Disney programs on the VCR. All the children are fascinated by Norma's two parrots. They especially like to handle the tame little parrot. Norma teaches them how to be gentle with the parrots and her other animals.

10:00 A.M.–11:00 A.M. Most days the children are able to play outside. Much of their play centers around the large two-story playhouse Norma designed and had built. They also are able to enjoy playing with Norma's two lop-eared rabbits, a very big cat, and two puppies.

11:00 A.M.–12:00 P.M. The children return inside to work on age-appropriate activities with Norma's helper. They will usually hear stories, sing songs, and do some preschool readiness activities.

12:00 P.M.–1:00 P.M. The children have their lunch after washing up from their outdoor time.

1:00 P.M.–3:00 P.M. All the children have a rest time. The younger children nap.

3:00 P.M.–5:00 P.M. The children play inside and outside under Norma's watchful eyes until they are picked up by their parents. A few children will remain after 5:00 P.M. because their parents commute or work late.

FOSTER CARE HOME PROGRAMS

While family child care home providers give home care to children when their parents are working, foster parents care for children in their homes around the clock for days, weeks, and months. The children have been placed in foster care because their own families cannot provide adequate care for them. Foster children are of all ages, from newborns to teenagers. All of the children have suffered the trauma of being separated from their parents, and many have been in several foster homes. Frequently, they have been abused or neglected by their parents. They may be malnourished or ill. Some have problems with schoolwork. Others are immature and do not relate well to their peers. Foster children require special help physically, mentally, socially, and emotionally. They need guidance and affection from mature adults in a solid home environment. Foster children especially need to develop a sense of security and healthy self-esteem. Foster care ends when a child reaches age eighteen.

The demand for foster parents is enormous in every area of the United States and Canada and is steadily growing even greater. The foster care systems of both countries are overwhelmed by the number of children needing care. Much of the increased demand for foster care homes can be attributed to the rising level of substance abuse by parents.

What Being a Foster Parent Is Like

Not everyone is cut out to be a foster parent. The personal demands are great. A concern and affection for children is absolutely essential, as are the necessary skills, stamina, and patience to deal with children who often have serious problems. Foster parents must be able to accept the temporariness of their jobs. They play a critical role in working toward the reunification of the children with their families, or when this is impossible, in helping the children to adjust to a permanent placement. In addition, foster parents need to work well as part of a team that includes social workers, court representatives, counselors, and health care professionals.

In order to be a foster parent, it is essential to obtain a state or provincial foster care license. It will set the number of foster children that a home can care for based on the number of beds, bedrooms, and the ages of the children. Even though licensing requirements will vary between the states and provinces, they usually include the following guidelines:

- Foster parents need to be over age twenty-one. They can be single or married.

- Foster parents must have sufficient income to support their own families without relying on foster care payments. Both parents can work if it does not adversely affect the care of the foster child.
- Foster parents must be fingerprinted and pass a criminal background check plus a general character interview.
- Foster parents need to have good health and the stamina to deal with the problems of foster children.
- Foster parents need to provide solid references.

Help Is Available for Foster Parents

Foster parents do not face the enormous problems of helping foster children alone. Whether they work for a public or private agency, they will attend orientation meetings to acquaint them with what foster parenting is like. In-service training will prepare them to work with foster children. And there will be newsletters continually updating them on all the services available to foster parents. Once they are on the job, there are continuing workshops for foster parents plus classes at community colleges. In addition, most foster parents join local associations that meet monthly to discuss mutual problems and to hear speakers on subjects involving foster parenting skills. These groups offer an excellent opportunity to network with other foster parents. Furthermore, each child's caseworker visits the child and the home regularly and assists the foster parents in helping the child. Special help is also available from counselors, health care professionals, and the state and provincial social services departments in the United States and Canada, respectively.

The Rewards of Foster Parenting

Foster parents receive a monthly payment for each child, which is designed to cover food, clothing, and recreation. Medical care is typically paid for by the state. If a child remains with a family for a year, the parents can receive a tax break by counting the child as a dependent. The foster parent program is not designed to offer any more financial remuneration than the cost of caring for a child or children. Similar benefits are available to Canadian foster parents.

The rewards of being a foster parent lie in the satisfaction of helping children who are desperately in need of a stable home life. Foster parents lend a helping hand to children when this assistance is needed. They have the gratification of making a difference, often a profound difference, in a child's life.

Profile of Foster Parents

Steve Warga and his wife, Karen, are licensed to care for five children in their home. They are currently foster parents to four children. In the three years that they have been caring for foster children, they have had seven children in their home. Steve works outside the home, but his wife is a full-time caregiver of the children, who are typically newborns to three-year-olds. All of the children for whom they have cared have had parents with substance abuse problems. Most of the children had been in several foster care homes before they came to the Wargas'. Their first foster child, who was four years old, had already been in four foster homes. His sister, who was five-and-a-half, had been in five homes in the two-and-a-half years before she came to the Wargas'. The Wargas are going to adopt these children. Another child came to them as a premature infant of a substance-abusing parent. Today, that child is healthy and will soon leave their home. Another brother and sister only stayed at their home for a short time because their parents were able to turn their lives around and care successfully for their children. Unfortunately, not all foster children return to parents who can give them the needed care. One of the toddlers for whom the Wargas are now caring will probably be placed permanently in their home since the mother has shown no concern about the child.

Steve points out several things that prospective foster parents should know. First of all, foster parents do not have to accept all children. They have the right to know about a child's background and to see a child before making a decision to have the child in their home. He also says that foster parents must work closely together to devise ways to handle these children. Many of the children who have been assigned to their care have been hyperactive, a condition that requires very skilled parenting. Finally, Steve admits that though foster parenting is challenging because the children need a high level of care, the opportunity to really help a child brings immense rewards.

ANOTHER CAREER POSSIBILITY: GROUP HOME CARE

Throughout the United States and Canada, groups of children are cared for in homes and on the grounds of residential centers in cottages or in large buildings. The children in these homes may be foster children or children with serious disabilities. Child care workers are needed in all of these facilities. In many cases, the workers are expected to act in a parental role. This means they will share a family life with a small group of children. They will see that the children do routine tasks in the home, help them with their homework, and try to make the children feel comfortable, secure, and cared for. At times, a married couple may work together in a group home. There are also group homes in which child care workers do not play a parental role but rather care for the children under the direction of a supervisor.

The demand for child care workers in group homes is high because the pay is usually low and the work can be very difficult in homes where the children have serious problems. Workers typically receive room and board at residential facilities and often will have paid vacations, health insurance, and other benefits.

THE REWARDS OF CARING FOR CHILDREN IN A HOME SETTING

Caring for children in one's home lets caregivers help the children of working parents develop in a home environment. At the same time, home caregivers have the pleasure of establishing a business in their own homes while contributing to the well-being of a future generation. Foster parents and group home workers have the reward of providing a helping hand to children when it is really needed. All child care workers have the satisfaction of enriching the lives of children.

CHAPTER

5

WORKING AS A NANNY

The television viewing audience has become far better acquainted recently with the profession of nanny through watching real-life nannies turn around families with poorly behaved children in just a week. It's rather like seeing the "practically perfect" Mary Poppins in action. While TV nannies have brought attention to this profession, it is definitely not a new one. The original nannies were trained in England at the Norland Institute. On the job, they wore starched brown uniforms with white aprons, little brown hats, and sensible, sturdy shoes. Much has changed since then. Today's nannies receive their formal training in community and nanny colleges and dress casually for work in jeans and sneakers. While Mary Poppins, the well-known fictional nanny, flew through the air with the Banks children, nannies are now found skateboarding with their charges.

NEED FOR NANNIES SKYROCKETS

U.S. News and World Report has described "nanny" as a "hot Job Track," where demand really outstrips supply, especially in major metropolitan areas. It is also an appealing job because it can offer such benefits as good pay, an opportunity to travel, paid vacations, use of a car, and health insurance. Read the following advertisements from the classified sections of newspapers and online employment websites, and note the range of positions open for employment as a nanny:

NANNY—Loving, exp'd, responsible. M–F. 3 young children. No housework. Health insurance. 30-hour week. 317-555-9872.

Nanny—Part time. Needed for daughters ages 12 and 14. Evenings and weekends. Own transportation and references req'd. Leave message. 212-555-0986.

Nanny—Needed for professional couple. Care for newborn. Transport 2 year old to and from preschool. Must be able to work 10-hour days (M–F). 612-555-4000.

Nanny—Needed M–F 6 A.M.–4 P.M. for quiet 5-year-old girl. Experience and references required. 703-555-2163 after 6 P.M.

Nanny—Must be willing to travel abroad. Twin 5-year-old boys. Contact travelingfamily@nannyhelpwanted.com.

Nanny—Two kids. Girl 4, boy 20 months. Four 10-hour days. Competitive pay. Generous benefits. Must drive. busyfamily@nannyhelpwanted.com.

NANNIES ARE NOT BABYSITTERS

Nannies have far greater responsibilities than babysitters. They are filling in for parents all day—not for just a few hours—and play a vital role in the family support system. Unlike babysitters, they may live in with a family. Plus, they will have a much longer workweek of from forty to sixty hours. Like babysitters, most nannies are females; however, there are a few male nannies. Tom Cruise hired a male nanny.

PREREQUISITES FOR BEING A NANNY

The International Nanny Association has adopted minimum standards for nannies specifying that a nanny must be at least eighteen years of age, have completed high school or the equivalent, and be in good general health, with proof of immunizations and, where required, negative TB test and/or chest x-ray. The one qualification that all nannies must also have is genuine respect for and devotion to children. The association also lists the following skills that nannies need to have:

- The ability to work in isolation without the support of coworkers
- The ability to handle new and different surroundings

- Knowledge of the basics of taking care of the physical and emotional needs of infants and young children
- The ability to handle an emergency
- Basic knowledge of child development
- Good communication skills
- The ability to be organized

In addition, families expect nannies to have no history of alcohol or drug abuse and a safe driving record and almost always prefer a nanny who does not smoke. And of course, it certainly helps if a nanny has a sense of humor.

A NANNY'S DUTIES

The job description for a nanny will obviously vary from household to household. In general, nannies have the following responsibilities, according to the International Nanny Association:

- Tending to the child's basic daily physical needs
- Meal planning and preparation
- Laundry and clothing care
- Organization of play activities and outings
- Discipline
- Intellectual stimulation
- Language activities
- Transportation

Any housekeeping responsibilities nannies may have are related primarily to the care of the children.

ON THE JOB WITH A NANNY

No two nannies will spend their time in exactly the same way. Observing how one nanny spent her day caring for three young children—Mary (7), John (5), and Larry (3)—will give you an idea of what this job can be like:

7:00 A.M. Start work.

7:05 A.M. See that Mary gets on the school bus.

7:30 A.M.–9 A.M. Feed the boys. See that they get dressed. Children then watch television. Help John with kindergarten speech. The children help clean up the house.

9:00 A.M.–10:30 A.M. Go to the park first, and then to the library to choose books.

10:30 A.M.–11:00 A.M. Prepare lunch for the boys. Make sure John is ready for kindergarten.

11:00 A.M.–12:30 P.M. Feed the children. Walk John to kindergarten.

12:30 P.M.–2:30 P.M. Read to Larry. Larry rests. Do laundry and other household tasks.

2:30 P.M.–3:00 P.M. Visit with Mary, who has returned from school.

3:00 P.M.–3:30 P.M. John returns home. Serve afternoon snack to children.

3:30 P.M.–4:30 P.M. The children do their chores and homework. Mary practices piano.

4:30 P.M.–6:30 P.M. The children play during the next two hours with some supervision. Dinner is prepared.

6:30 P.M. Family meal.

7:00 P.M. Day is finished.

PROFILE OF A NANNY

As a college student, Sarah Wegert was asked to babysit for a family during her spring break. Although it meant that Sarah would spend her spring break at home in Vail, Colorado, Sarah agreed to help the family who was visiting from Chicago. Sarah quickly bonded with the family and their three young girls, and was asked to nanny for the family for six weeks in the summer back at their home in Chicago. Because Sarah had family in Chicago, she felt comfortable accepting the job.

That summer, Sarah moved in with the family, who provided her with a car, mobile phone, gas, and spending money. Sarah's day typically began around noon when she picked the children up from their activities. The young girls and Sarah would spend the remainder of the day together, riding bikes, going to the pool, or visiting museums in Chicago. Sarah was asked to rejoin the family the next summer, and she agreed. During her second summer with the family, Sarah joined them on their family vacation to Sydney, Australia for the Olympics. The family provided all accommodations and Olympic tickets for Sarah, and she helped watch the children during the trip.

Sarah enjoyed her experience the most because of the strong connection she made with the family. She said, "They made me feel a part of the family." Sarah continues to speak with the family and visits them when she is in Chicago with her family. While she had never been a nanny before, Sarah felt prepared because of her many years of babysitting. According to Sarah, a good nanny must enjoy playing with children, be flexible, and feel comfortable working (maybe even living) with a family. Today, Sarah is a third- grade teacher in Colorado.

NANNY CODE OF CONDUCT

The International Nanny Association has adopted a Code of Conduct to promote professionalism and ethical practices among nannies, educators, and those who employ and place in-home child care specialists. By virtue of their membership in the International Nanny Association, members agree to abide by this Code of Conduct and to support quality in-home child care for the world's most valuable resources—our children.

Responsibilities to the Child
A nanny shall:

- Respect each child as a human being and never knowingly participate in any practice that is disrespectful, dangerous, exploitive, intimidating, or psychologically or physically harmful.
- Maintain a safe and healthy atmosphere that encourages optimum social, emotional, intellectual, and physical development of children.

- Provide various learning opportunities through which a child can explore and utilize his or her continued personal growth and development.
- Recognize the unique potential of each child, encourage questions, and present answers that children can understand.
- Keep abreast of current activity in the areas of childhood development through continued education, either formally or informally.
- Work toward promoting knowledge and understanding of young children and their needs and act as an advocate for children's rights.
- Be familiar with the signs of child abuse and neglect and be knowledgeable of procedures for dealing with them.

Responsibilities to the Parents

A nanny shall:

- Treat parents and other family members with respect by maintaining confidentiality and respecting the family's right to privacy.
- Work together with parents to create an environment conducive to the healthy development of the child.
- Respect the family's child-rearing values and parents' rights to make decisions for their children.
- Support the family value system, cultural expression, and individual characteristics and refrain from imposing personal values or biases on the child.
- Be an advocate for children and work to protect their rights.
- Not hold the child accountable for negative interactions between parents and nanny.
- Inform parents of physical injury, illness, and emotional crises should they occur in the child's life.

Responsibilities to Self

A nanny shall:

- Present herself/himself as an acceptable adult role model, take pride in personal appearance and professional behavior, and refrain from activity that might injure credibility or produce a negative representation of herself/himself or an employer.

- Continue to improve personal knowledge of child development by seeking contemporary information through formal and informal means, such as membership in child care organizations.

NANNY SUPPORT GROUPS

The three nannies whose careers are described later in this chapter often arrange playdates for their charges. Besides giving the children an opportunity to play with other children, they also give the nannies an opportunity to share experiences and enjoy adult company. Nannies find it easy to meet other nannies at preschools, parks, and children's classes. There are also many nanny support groups which provide social opportunities, professional development, and networking opportunities. Visit nannynetwork.com to find where some of these support groups are located.

SALARY AND FRINGE BENEFITS

Nannies are the elite of child care workers and are enjoying rising wages. The actual salary that a nanny receives does vary widely based on where the nanny lives and the nanny's qualifications and experience. The 2006 salary survey of the International Nanny Association showed a range of weekly earnings from a low of $300 per week to a high of $1,000 per week. These results are shown in Table 5.1. Monthly salaries for live-in nannies in Canada vary from C$1,400 to C$2,000 while those for live-out nannies go from C$1,900 to C$3,000.

In addition to a salary, nannies may receive paid health insurance, room and board, a car to drive, travel to exotic vacation spots, membership in health clubs, and an opportunity to attend college part time. Some families even pay college tuition for their nannies. An International Nanny Association survey shows that more than half of all nannies receive paid sick days and national and religious holidays. About one-third of the surveyed nannies received two weeks paid vacation, use of an employer's vehicle, and paid personal days. Plus, 20 percent of the nannies received 100 percent employer paid health insurance.

Table 5.1   2006 Salary Survey

Percentage of Nannies Reporting	Earnings per Week
9	$300
5	$350
5	$450
8	$500
6	$550
8	$600
5	$650
4	$700
3	$750
4	$800
3	$1,000

Source: International Nanny Association

WHAT IT TAKES TO BECOME A NANNY

The International Nanny Association strongly supports specialized training for nannies who care for children in an in-home setting. Prospective nannies should contact this international network of nannies, nanny placement agency owners, nanny educators, and nanny employers for career information. Write to International Nanny Association, 2020 Southwest Freeway, Suite 208, Houston, TX 77098, or go online to nanny.org.

Required Competencies

Through education, nannies can acquire the competencies needed to provide quality child care and a nurturing environment for all children. The International Nanny Association specifically recommends that a nanny demonstrate the ability to perform competently in the following areas:

- Observe and assess the behavior of children
- Plan and implement consistent daily routines

- Create an environment to foster trust, self-esteem, and independence in children
- Use age-appropriate behavior management techniques in interaction with children
- Plan and implement developmentally appropriate play/learning activities for children
- Choose and care for developmentally appropriate play materials and equipment

Competencies related to interaction with parents/employers and to family dynamics:

- Communicate effectively, both orally and in writing
- Articulate a personal philosophy of child care
- Maintain the confidentiality of the employing family
- Demonstrate knowledge and understanding of parents'/employer's philosophy of child rearing and recognize the special role a nanny assumes in becoming a part of the child-rearing "team"
- Recognize the ultimate authority of parents in making decisions regarding the welfare and care of the child
- Follow instructions and directions in a timely manner

Competencies related to professionalism, personal development, and social skills:

- Present a professional attitude and appearance
- Use good judgment
- Use appropriate language and manners
- Demonstrate initiative in planning and performance of tasks and an ability to work unsupervised
- Participate in social, cultural, and educational activities to enhance personal growth and maintain and improve competency

Competencies related to the physical care of children:

- Perform tasks related to the physical care of children
- Maintain appropriate hygienic standards for children regarding bathing, hand washing, and care of the hair and teeth

- Feed, change, and bathe infants
- Prepare infant feedings and care for feeding equipment
- Select clothing appropriate to the child's physical/social activities
- Plan and supervise rest, bed, and nap times
- Plan and prepare nutritionally balanced meals and snacks
- Care for the mildly ill child
- Recognize symptoms of common childhood illnesses
- Keep accurate records
- Perform appropriate first-aid techniques
- Handle emergency situations
- Observe appropriate safety precautions when traveling with children

Competencies related to domestic tasks and care of the child's environment:

- Perform domestic tasks related to care and maintenance of the child's areas of the home such as bedrooms, playrooms, bathrooms, and outside play space
- Launder and make simple repairs to children's clothing
- Observe safety precautions appropriate to a private home

International Nanny Credential Exam

The INA Nanny Credential Exam was created as a way to measure a nanny's working knowledge in the following areas:

Child Development
Family/Provider Communication
Child Guidance
Multicultural/Diversity Awareness
Learning Environment
Personal Qualities of a Nanny
Safety
Management Skills
Health
Nutrition
Professionalism

Because the exam is challenging, it is strongly recommended that anyone sitting for the exam has a minimum of 2,000 hours of professional child care experience and current certification in infant/child CPR and first aid. After the exam is scored, nannies who pass will be given a certificate that can be added to his/her portfolio or résumé.

Nanny Training Programs

There are several approaches to acquiring the formal training nannies need. Some nannies obtain associate or bachelor's degrees in early childhood education. Many attend training programs in private schools, vocational schools, and community colleges. Typical nanny training programs offer a variety of courses related to children and child care. There are courses in child growth and development, psychology, food and nutrition, health and safety, play activities, first aid, cardiopulmonary resuscitation (CPR), and family dynamics. The programs often include hands-on care of children. Many schools provide the future nanny with information on personal health and grooming, etiquette, social skills, and professional development. Nannies who do not have formal training should have babysitting or day-care experience or have raised their own families.

A Public College Program

Vincennes University in Vincennes, Indiana, has a professional nanny program. The program is a one-year, certificate degree program and requires completion of thirty-one credit hours. Figure 5.1 shows the actual curriculum as it appears in the college catalog.

Choosing a Nanny School

The International Nanny Association publishes the *Annual Directory of Nanny Training Programs, Nanny Placement Agencies and Special Services.* The book's section on schools has information about the length of training programs, program costs, admission requirements, and availability of financial aid for schools that meet the association's requirements.

Before enrolling in a nanny school, prospective nannies should carefully check out the merits of the school's program, according to Joy Shelton, former chairperson of the American Council of Nanny Schools.

Figure 5.1   Vincennes University

FAMILY AND CONSUMER SCIENCES–PROFESSIONAL NANNY CERTIFICATE 2305
A One-Year Certificate of Graduation Program
Professional Nanny Certificate • Nanny Certificate • Family and Consumer Sciences: Professional Nanny Certificate

Intensive training program for Child Care Professionals who will enter family homes and share in the responsibility of rearing their children. This program prepares students to meet the varied needs of the families they serve and integrate their lives with those of their employers. These duties could include adapting menus to special dietary needs, managing the day-to-day affairs of the household, aiding a handicapped or gifted child, and communicating with schools, parents, and children.

Students who wish to continue their education find that the Child Care Professional Nanny Certificate is the first step in their career ladder. These credits received at Vincennes University can be applied toward an associate's degree. This training can often be applied toward a degree in teaching or other child care professions.

Upon successful completion of 31 semester hours of specified courses, students will receive a certificate of accreditation as a Child Care Professional Nanny from VU.

Credit Hours:

ARTT	104	Design in Materials	3
ENGL	101	English Composition I	3
FACS	130	Infant, Toddler, and Child Care	3
FACS	132	The Nanny as a Professional	1
FACS	137	Home Management and Family Communications	3
FACS	140	Field Placement I	2
FACS	141	Field Placement Seminar I	1
FACS	142	Field Placement II	2
FACS	143	Field Placement Seminar II	1
FACS	156	Marriage and the Family	3
FACS	207	Nutrition for Child Care Administration and Educators	3
FACS	211	Food Preparation and Nutrition Laboratory	1
HLTH	211	First Aid	2
PSYC	141	Applied Psychology -or-	
PSYC	142	General Psychology	3
			31

NOTE: All students must satisfy the University's minimum requirements through either placement tests or enrollment in MATH 011, MATH 103, 105, or 109. It is highly recommended that students achieve Red Cross life saving certification or intermediate swimming proficiency.

She offers the following suggestions on how a program should be assessed:

1. Talk to graduates.
2. Talk to families that have hired students from the school.
3. Check with the Better Business Bureau and local chamber of commerce to make sure that no complaints about the school have been received.
4. Check with the state's department of education to determine if the school has a license.
5. Find out if the school is accredited.

The International Nanny Association lists these questions for prospective nannies to ask about a training program:

1. What specific courses does the nanny program curriculum include?
2. If the program requires work with children as part of the training, is the work supervised by an instructor?
3. Is the program accredited by a federally approved accrediting body?
4. What are the qualifications of the instructors?
5. How many students have completed the training program? Were they able to find jobs as nannies?
6. Is it possible to visit the school or sit in on a class?
7. What is the tuition refund policy if the student drops out of the course? Can the course work be transferred to another school or program?
8. Is counseling or tutoring available to the student who may be having trouble with the program?
9. What percentage of students who sign up for the program complete it?

APPLYING TO A NANNY SCHOOL

Nanny schools are looking for candidates who have the backgrounds, interests, and experiences that will enable them to become excellent nannies after training. Most use a screening process to make sure that enrollees do not have a criminal record or their name on a child abuse registry. In addition, the schools are looking for candidates with an above-average driving record, a clean drug and alcohol record, and no medical disabilities that would prevent them in any way from caring for their charges. Physically, they should be able to stoop, kneel, crouch, and crawl. Good vision and hearing are necessary, as well as being able to lift fifty pounds. On the personality side, schools want prospective students to demonstrate creativity, time management skills, initiative, responsibility, self-confidence, and a love of teaching and children.

FINDING EMPLOYMENT AS A NANNY

Nannies can find jobs through newspaper advertisements, the Internet, and referrals from friends. However, the International Nanny Association suggests that nannies rely on their training school placement bureaus and nanny placement agencies to avoid negative experiences. Placement agencies match the nanny's qualifications and preferences with the needs of families searching for nannies. The family, not the nanny, is charged for the placement service. The National Alliance of Professional Nanny Agencies (APNA) is an alliance of agencies that promotes best business practices in all areas of nanny placement. Visit the organization's website at theapna.org to search for an agency.

A nanny agency typically requires nannies to complete an application, supply references, and have an interview with agency personnel. According to the International Nanny Association, this process may also involve taking fingerprints and checking to see whether the nanny has a criminal record or bad driving record. The prospective nanny may also be required to take a blood test and tuberculosis test and may be requested to provide a physician's statement certifying that the nanny is in good health and free of contagious diseases. In the United States, it is also essential to prove U.S. citizenship or eligibility to work legally in the country.

Profile of a Midwestern Placement Agency

This agency acts as a go-between, screening both clients and nannies to get the perfect fit. At no cost to the nanny, the agency will give the nanny a physical exam, a tuberculosis test, and a drug test; in addition, the agency will arrange for fingerprint, criminal background, and driving record checks and will train the nanny in CPR.

To be eligible for placement by this agency, nannies need to have two years of child care experience or a two-year associate's degree. If this requirement is met, and after satisfactorily completing preliminary applications, the nanny will fill out the application shown in Figure 5.2.

Figure 5.2   Nanny Agency Application

Application

Please type or print clearly.   Date _____

PERSONAL INFORMATION   Referral Source _____

Name _____ Social Security # _____

Home Address _____ Phone # _____

City _____ State _____Zip _____

Are you 18 years or older? _____   Drivers License # _____

EMPLOYMENT DESIRED

	Date you	Salary
Position _____	can start _____	desired _____

Do you desire: Full-time _____   Part-time _____

Summer Only _____   Live-In _____   Live-Out _____

EDUCATION
List high schools, colleges, or other training.

Name/Location	Dates Attended	Graduate?	Major

GENERAL

Special Skills _____

Hobbies/Interests _____

Are you certified in CPR/First Aid ? _____ When _____

_____

PLEASE COMPLETE THE BACK OF THIS APPLICATION

Figure 5.2   Nanny Agency Application (continued)

FORMER EMPLOYERS

List below last four employers, starting with last one.

Name/Location	Dates From-To	Position	Reason for Leaving

REFERENCES

Give the names of three persons not related to you, whom you have known at least one year.

Name	Address	Phone	Years Known

List all child care experience: _____

_____

Please read the following carefully; sign and date.

I certify that the facts contained in this application are true and complete to the best of my knowledge and understand that, if employed, falsified statements on this application will cancel placement.

I authorize investigation of all statements contained herein and the references listed above to give you any and all information concerning my previous employment and any pertinent information they may have, and release all parties from all liability for any damages that may result from furnishing same to you.

I understand and agree that, if hired, my employment is for no definite period and may, regardless of the date of payment of my wages and salary, be terminated at any time without prior notice and without cause.

Signature _____   Date _____

An agency requirement. This agency also requires all nannies to write a "Dear Parent" letter to introduce themselves to parents who might wish to interview them. The following letter was written by a prospective nanny named Linette:

Dear Parent,

Hi, my name is Linette. I am a 24-year-old single female with caring, honest, and reliable attributes. I am laid-back and flexible and try to possess an open mind at all times. Some of my interests include working out, walking, reading, and participating in outdoor activities. I have learned to be very creative when it comes to free time. I am always eager to try new activities and have a desire to learn. I am hoping to obtain a live-in nanny position in which two or three toddlers are involved. I prefer ages 1 and above but would not turn down an opportunity in which an infant was involved.

I recently received my B.S. in sociology with a minor in criminal justice. I graduated in December 20__ from Iowa State University in Ames, Iowa. During my studies at Iowa State, I had the opportunity to enroll in child development classes. I learned a lot about toddlers and the different stages of development they go through. I truly enjoyed these classes, and I am hoping to pursue a career involving toddlers. My future plans include returning to college to obtain my master's degree in early childhood or family and marriage counseling.

My work history has allowed me to gain valuable experience. I have learned to work as a team member and how to accept responsibility for my own actions. My communication skills have improved due to the amount of interaction I have had with various people. Employers and coworkers have often complimented me on my ability to be efficient, confident, and dependable. Although my job experiences do not directly involve children, I feel you will be able to develop a good idea of what kind of employee I would be. As far as experience with children, I come from a family with five brothers and six sisters. I fall right in the middle. Therefore, I have had lots of experience with my six younger brothers and sisters. During grade school and high school, I have also had various babysitting jobs. I would be more than happy to provide you with the names of these people. With all this behind me, I feel I am well qualified for commitment to your family.

I sincerely hope you will consider me for an interview with you and your family. I strongly believe I will be a positive role model for your children.

Thank you for your time and consideration.

Interviewing for a Nanny Position

Part of the process of obtaining a nanny position is being interviewed by prospective employers. The previously mentioned midwestern agency holds interviews in which clients talk to nannies selected by the agency. Each interview is scheduled for approximately thirty minutes. Here is a list of the questions that parents are given to help them interview nannies, and prospective nannies should be expecting to answer:

1. What is your best quality?
2. Are you flexible?
3. Are you punctual?
4. What is your approach to discipline?
5. How many children do you feel comfortable caring for?
6. What ages of children do you prefer?
7. Tell me about your experiences with children. What did you like most? Least?
8. How long of a commitment can you make?
9. How assertive are you?
10. Are you willing to care for children according to my philosophies?
11. What are some of the activities you would like to do with children?
12. If you took them on field trips, where would you like to go?
13. How do you react to criticism?
14. Tell me about your background.
15. Do you know how to childproof a home?
16. Do you know the Heimlich maneuver?
17. Do you feel comfortable driving with children in the car?
18. What hours can you work?
19. Can you work overtime? Weekends? Travel with our family on vacation?
20. What are your feelings about doing light housework?
21. What do you consider light housework to be?
22. Why do you want to be a nanny?
23. How many days did you miss from your job last year?

At this agency, clients usually find a nanny from the first group of interviews. If not, three additional nannies will be chosen for interviews. The agency always suggests that a second interview be held in the client's home so the client can see how the nanny interacts with the children. The agency advises both clients and nannies that if either has any apprehension about the other, no commitments should be made. If a perfect match is made, both nanny and client return to the office to negotiate a contract. It is important that both parties understand the job. Everything must be spelled out clearly in the contract. The contract shown in Figure 5.3 demonstrates what is involved in nanny/client contracts.

The midwestern agency gives its clients a thirty-day trial period. If the relationship between nanny and family does not work out during this time, the agency will locate a new home for the nanny and a new nanny for the family.

THREE NANNIES TELL ABOUT THEIR BACKGROUNDS AND FIRST JOBS

In all professions, individuals may arrive at the same position in different ways. The following stories of three much sought after nannies on the Upper East Side in New York City exemplify this. Each took a different route to becoming a nanny, but all share a love of children and an ability to rear children according to their parents' wishes.

Ottie was an office employee who felt it would be more interesting to work with children. She went through a short child care program learning more about what children are like and how to relate to people of different cultures. Her first job was obtained through an agency.

Sandra was a stay-at-home mom whose experience in child care came from raising her own child. This was her training for becoming a nanny. She got her first job through word of mouth. A friend of a friend mentioned that someone was looking for a nanny. She obtained her next job by placing an ad on the Internet on a nanny help wanted website.

Ishar had worked as a cashier and cake decorator before becoming a nanny. She also had raised two children. Ishar began working in child care as a babysitter. While working at this job, she went to informal classes where nannies and babysitters would learn about child development and the teacher would help them resolve problems that they were having on the job. Ishar has also taken two CPR classes. Her first nanny job was obtained through an agency, while her current job came about because a parent had seen how well she handled children in her first job and asked her to work for her family.

Figure 5.3   Employer/Nanny Contract

EMPLOYER/NANNY

This agreement is entered into between _____
(employer)

and _____.
(nanny)

The employer seeks to secure the nanny as a professional child caregiver, and nanny wishes to provide such services.

Employer's Address _____ Telephone _____

_____ Zip Code _____

Employer's Child(ren) Name _____ Age _____

Name _____ Age _____

Name _____ Age _____

Nanny's Address _____ Telephone _____

_____ Zip Code _____

Nanny's Social Security Number _____

Nanny's Compensation: Salary _____ /Hrly _____

Overtime Pay _____ Holiday Pay _____

Scheduled Hours _____ Days _____

Nanny is to receive _____ Vacation Days

Paid Vacation Yes _____ No_____   Paid Holidays Yes _____ No _____

Nanny is to receive the following holidays _____

_____

DUTIES:

Child Care _____

Household _____

Errands _____

Transporting _____

Other _____

TERMINATION:

Nanny agrees to pay the employer $_____ if the nanny quits before

_____. The nanny will give _____ weeks notice prior

to leaving employment. Employer will give nanny _____ weeks notice and

$_____ severance pay to terminate agreement.

Nanny's Signature _____ Date _____

Employer's Signature _____ Date _____

THE AU PAIR EXPERIENCE

Nannies are take-charge people who are completely responsible for the care of children. Au pairs also live with families and provide help with child care and light housework. They usually work under the direct supervision of the parent and may or may not have previous child care experience. Au pairs will work from forty to sixty hours a week. Besides American au pairs, there are foreign au pairs who live in the United States for up to a year to experience American life. They live as part of the host family and receive a small allowance/salary in exchange for help with child care and housework. Americans can also work abroad as au pairs, usually in Europe, to experience the culture of another country.

THE REWARDS OF BEING A NANNY

The care of children in a home setting can be a rewarding career. Nannies are able to provide children with the nurturing care they need; in return, the nannies will receive love and affection from the children as well as high regard from their families. Today's nannies provide the high-quality in-home care that parents are seeking and receive respect as well-trained professionals.

C H A P T E R

WORKING AS A BABYSITTER

Almost every parent has a need for a babysitter either occasionally or on a regular basis. There is always a very high demand for and low supply of babysitters, especially for special occasions. Many child care providers began their careers as babysitters. While most babysitters are teenagers, many are adults who work in the children's home or their own homes on a part-time or full-time basis.

Even though there are no licensing or training requirements for this job, the more skilled babysitters are, the more clients they have, and the more money they earn. Well-qualified babysitters know the importance of learning all they can about taking care of children. They must be ready to perform cardiopulmonary resuscitation (CPR) in an emergency, handle a child with a sore throat, or treat a sprained finger. These skills are learned through classes at YMCAs or YWCAs, high schools, vocational schools, and community colleges, and through the American and Canadian Red Cross.

LEARNING BABYSITTING SKILLS

Taking classes and learning how to care for children is no guarantee that a prospective babysitter will be an excellent one. Certain special qualifications are needed. Babysitters need to have patience to play endless games with children. They should truly enjoy being around children, whether the children are crying babies or rambunctious youngsters. Furthermore, babysitters need to be confident that they can handle children ranging in age from infant to preteen. Finally, having a cool head in a crisis is an absolutely essential skill, as babysitters must remain calm in emergencies.

Child care classes do give practical training in health and safety and important information about child development. They provide instruction on how to prevent injuries and reduce the spread of infectious diseases. In these classes, babysitters and other child care providers learn how to recognize and care for common childhood illnesses. They also find out how to improve their skills in communicating with children and their parents.

American Red Cross Child Care Course

The American Red Cross has produced, in cooperation with the American Academy of Pediatrics and with review from the National Academy of Sciences, the first and only national program designed for child care providers. The child care course is taught by a certified instructor who presents the information in an easy-to-follow format through group discussions, videos, demonstrations, role playing, and short lectures. At the conclusion of the course, participants take a handy, attractive workbook to serve as a ready resource when they are caring for young children.

The Red Cross presents their child care course in seven units:

1. Preventing Childhood Injuries
2. Infant and Child First Aid
3. Caring for Ill Children
4. Preventing Infectious Diseases
5. Learning About Child Development
6. Communicating with Children and Parents
7. Recognizing and Reporting Child Abuse

This course takes fifteen hours to complete. The first eight hours are devoted to pediatric CPR and first aid. Participants earning 80 percent or better on the written CPR test receive certification in CPR for one year. Those passing the first-aid test with 80 percent or better earn first-aid certification for two years. The remaining seven hours of the course are devoted to preventive health and safety. For satisfactorily completing this part of the course, participants receive a certificate.

Babysitting Courses

The Red Cross also has a babysitting course designed for eleven- to fifteen-year-olds. It helps them learn how to:

1. Interview for a babysitting job
2. Choose safe and age-appropriate toys and games
3. Perform first aid
4. Learn diapering and feeding techniques
5. Handle bedtime issues
6. Have a safe babysitting experience

Canadian Red Cross

The Canadian Red Cross also has a babysitting course for adolescents of eleven years old or older. They learn valuable tips for managing business as well as:

- Important child care skills
- Safety tips for children of all ages
- How to cope with common problems, like tantrums
- What to do if anything makes the babysitter uncomfortable
- Some great games and other ideas for having fun while babysitting
- How to make the children's environment safe
- What are the respective rights and responsibilities of babysitter and the family hiring one

In addition, the Red Cross has courses that are appropriate for older adults who wish to acquire or improve their babysitting skills. These include injury prevention, first-aid training, and CPR training.

Safety Courses

The U.S. Consumer Product Safety Commission has produced an informational pamphlet, "The Super Sitter," in order to help babysitters protect their young charges from unreasonable risks of injury and death associated with consumer products. It can be obtained online at cpsc.gov. For adolescent babysitters, Safe Sitters® offers a course to keep children safe and sound. See the Appendix for contact information.

BABYSITTERS NEED TO BE AWARE OF HOW CHILDREN DEVELOP

Unless babysitters understand what young children can and cannot do at certain ages, they will not be able to understand the behavior of their charges or how to choose appropriate activities for them. In Chapter 2, a detailed list of the skills children should have acquired by the ages of fifteen months, two-and-a-half years, and five years are spelled out for ten important skill areas: listening, thinking, fine motor, social, self-help, self-esteem, speaking, prereading, math, and gross motor.

THE BABYSITTER'S RESPONSIBILITIES

Babysitters have several responsibilities from the moment they enter a home. Their major responsibility will be to watch the children, which includes:

- Playing with the children
- Preventing accidents
- Selecting safe and appropriate toys and games for each child
- Giving the children their undivided attention
- Changing diapers of infants and toddlers
- Bathing and dressing infants and young children
- Feeding babies
- Fixing meals or snacks for the children
- Cleaning up messes
- Handling the household

If a babysitting job is going to be long-term, the babysitter must meet with families ahead of time to establish their guidelines and expectations. On first-time assignments as well as subsequent jobs, babysitters need to secure five vital pieces of information before the parents leave:

1. General behavior guidelines
2. Rules on television viewing and snacking
3. The children's official bedtime

4. Special duties to be performed, such as bathing or feeding the children, doing dishes, etc.

5. A telephone number or information on how to reach the parents in case of an emergency

For all jobs, babysitters need to know where the following items are located in the home:

flashlight	vacuum cleaner
candles	paper towels
matches	writing paper
first-aid kit	pencils, pens
clock	tissues
cleaning supplies	telephone
sponge	thermostats

When babysitters watch children in their own homes, they have the additional responsibility of making their homes safe for children. This includes doing such things as:

- Keeping the home tidy
- Placing child-resistant covers on all electrical outlets
- Storing dangerous chemicals and all drugs out of children's reach
- Keeping firearms locked away
- Making sure cribs meet safety standards
- Safety-proofing stairs
- Installing toilet seat locks
- Keeping knives out of children's reach
- Storing tools, especially power tools, out of reach

Understanding That Families Are Different

All families do not have the same values. Babysitters need to ask questions to be sure that they understand the way that individual families want them to care for their children. They need to know about limitations on TV time and the types of programs that the children are allowed to watch. The same goes for watching videos and using the computer.

Also, they should know whether prayer is part of such rituals as eating or going to bed.

THE BUSINESS SIDE OF BABYSITTING

To avoid misunderstandings, business arrangements need to be discussed before babysitting for the first time. This includes discussing the fee before accepting an assignment, finding out how many hours the parents want the babysitter to work, transportation considerations, and whatever special chores the family wishes done outside of babysitting.

Most babysitters find jobs through people they know or by advertising their services on bulletin boards, in bulletins of churches and other local organizations, and in newspapers. Some babysitters work for agencies that will assign them to jobs. Earnings are based on community standards. A babysitter in New York City or Chicago will earn more than one in rural North Dakota. Earnings are typically an hourly fee. However, older, experienced babysitters will be able to charge more for their services than their younger, less experienced counterparts. Young beginning babysitters often start at $5.00 to $7.00 per hour while more experienced adult sitters will typically earn $10.00 to $25.00 per hour based on the number of children in a family. Overnight sitters often receive a flat fee.

The Flyer

Once babysitters become known for their expertise, they will usually be in great demand. At first, however, it may be necessary to do some marketing. Frequently, this is accomplished by handing out flyers or displaying them in places where parents are likely to see them. The flyer is rather like a mini-résumé and should include such information as: name, contact number or e-mail address, experience, child care or babysitting classes attended, pay rate, and availability of references.

HELPFUL HINTS FROM A YOUNG BABYSITTER

Jessica Donaldson, an eighth grader, has already been babysitting for more than three years. Starting at such a young age has become common because of the shortage of babysitters. Jessica does not establish a price with her clients. Instead, she feels that most people pay her a fair wage. The families that hire Jessica to babysit expect her to keep the children out of trouble and to clean up any messes made by the children. Jessica believes that the major task in babysitting is to keep all the children entertained. She always asks families to provide her with specific information about how to reach them, when they will be home, and special directions for mealtimes, bedtimes, and any medications that need to be given.

Jessica has solid advice for prospective babysitters. She advises them to begin by going on a job with an experienced sitter to see what the job entails. Jessica believes that babysitters need to prepare for this job by learning how to change diapers and finding out what kind of things children of different ages like to do. Also, it is important to keep babysitting fun for both the sitter and the children so it does not become a routine and boring job. Jessica points out that the test of being a successful babysitter is being asked back again and again because the children love to have you.

BABYSITTERS ARE IMPORTANT CAREGIVERS

Babysitters give parents worry-free workdays because they know their children are being carefully watched. They allow parents to have a few carefree hours of togetherness or a vacation without the company of their children. Children need trained, well-qualified babysitters to help them grow and develop into healthy, happy people when their parents cannot be with them. The job of babysitter is an important one.

CHAPTER

7

EDUCATING CHILDREN

The teaching profession is certainly one of the most important, for teachers have the responsibility of transmitting knowledge from one generation to the next. It was Christa McAuliffe, the teacher/astronaut, who summed this up by saying, "I touch the future, I teach." In this chapter, opportunities to teach children from preschool through middle school will be discussed. These are the formative years in which teachers affect how well children will succeed in later schooling and in their lives. Those who choose to become teachers are working in the largest profession in the world and are joining a long list of stellar names beginning with Socrates and Aristotle.

WHAT IT TAKES TO BE A TEACHER

While teaching children is a noble career, not everyone has the personality to be a teacher. Some teachers make learning come alive and inspire the children in their classes, while others produce monotonous lessons that bore their students. A successful teacher of children will have the following attributes:

- Enjoys being with children
- Is patient with children
- Keeps cool in trying situations involving children
- Gets satisfaction from helping children
- Has a pleasant-sounding voice
- Has a high energy level

- Is able to adapt to a new situation quickly
- Is able to control a group of children easily
- Is imaginative and creative
- Enjoys reading children's literature
- Enjoys playing with children
- Enjoys spontaneous activities
- Enjoys planning activities for children
- Is enthusiastic
- Is a self-starter
- Has a bit of a flair for acting
- Is open-minded
- Is organized

Anyone wanting to teach children should have most of these attributes in order to be well suited to this career.

CHILDREN'S FIRST TEACHERS

Children's first experience with school increasingly occurs when they enter preschool at the ages of three or four. No longer do parents wait until their children are kindergarten-age to introduce them to school. This is partially due to the pushing down of the first grade curriculum into kindergarten—thus necessitating more formal preparation for kindergarten. This doesn't mean teaching them to read or write or do workbook activities. Instead, it means helping children learn to get along in a classroom situation. They must be taught to listen attentively, to solve problems, to manipulate their hands effectively, to socialize with their classmates, to express themselves clearly, and to take care of their basic needs. Simultaneously, the preschool teacher must fan their desire to learn through interesting activities for groups and individuals. Good preschool teachers give young children a big boost up the school ladder of success. It is an excellent career consideration for prospective teachers who especially like young children.

Preparation for Becoming a Preschool Teacher

Employment requirements vary widely for preschool teachers. Most states and provinces require teachers to have a certificate to teach in a public preschool.

In the United States, these teachers usually have a four-year college degree in child development or early childhood education plus the necessary licenses. Preschool teachers at private schools usually face less stringent requirements. They may hold an associate's degree in early childhood education, as discussed in Chapter 3. Some enter the field through the Child Development Associate (CDA) program offered by the Council for Early Childhood Professional Recognition, also discussed in Chapter 3. In Canada, teachers in public schools are likely to hold an Early Childhood Education (ECE) diploma. In addition, preschool teachers can get training through the American and Canadian Montessori Societies, which offer many different programs. There are not usually specific qualifications for teaching in private preschools in either country.

What Being a Preschool Teacher Is Like

Long before the first child ever enters the classroom, preschool teachers have made preparations for the day. Lesson plans have been created describing what the children will do, storybooks have been selected, paints have been mixed, and craft projects have been set up. From the minute children walk through the classroom door, the teacher is busy greeting, guiding, assisting, and encouraging each individual student as well as organizing group activities. The teacher also has to spot children who are not feeling well, listen to complaints, and comfort the sad or injured child. Preschool teachers need to have an excellent understanding of children, how they develop, and their abilities at each age level. It is also essential that preschool teachers be capable of creating age-appropriate activities.

The Rewards of Teaching Preschool

Being a preschool teacher is immensely rewarding because these children really show affection for their teachers. Preschool teachers have the exceptional opportunity to fuel their students' energy and enthusiasm for future learning. The ability to start children off successfully on the educational path is satisfying.

Salary and Fringe Benefits

Preschool teachers' salaries are typically based on their education level and the number of years of teaching experience they have. At private schools, the rate of pay is often only an hourly wage. Preschool teachers in public schools receive the best pay. In general, the pay for preschool teachers is fairly low. In 2004, the median hourly earnings of preschool teachers was $9.34 in the United States. In Canada, preschool teachers averaged C$11.33 per hour in 2006.

Benefits for preschool teachers, such as health insurance and paid vacations, vary widely, with some private schools providing good benefits and others offering none at all. Teachers at this level, however, work relatively short hours. There is also the added bonus of having time off for all major holidays, plus a long summer vacation.

Profile of a Preschool Teacher

Cathy Johnson followed in the family tradition of teaching. Her mother taught at the first-grade level for forty-nine years. As she was growing up, Cathy observed her mother's love for teaching and saw the contribution to children's lives that her mother was making. To pursue her desired career as a preschool teacher, Cathy obtained a kindergarten endorsement and a master's degree in early childhood education.

Today, Cathy is a lead teacher in a preschool. She is responsible for selecting what will be taught in the classroom, planning how it will be taught, and teaching the lesson. In addition, Cathy has two aides who provide her with support in the classroom. Besides teaching, Cathy regularly holds conferences with parents and writes notes letting them know how their children are doing. Lead teachers also must handle the paperwork involved in running a class.

Cathy feels that a good preschool teacher must be patient and firm with his or her young students. At the same time, she says, it is necessary to be loving and very flexible. Cathy loves her job and says there are far more things she likes about it than she dislikes. Here are a few things Cathy likes about her job:

- It is never boring because there is so much variety.
- Each day at work is fun.
- She enjoys meeting the children's families and getting to know them well as she works closely with them.
- She has the opportunity to be creative throughout the work day.
- She likes working closely with her two aides, who help her keep the classroom running smoothly.

- The children constantly make her feel good because they genuinely like her.
- She does not have to spend much time keeping records, attending meetings, or writing reports.
- The shorter teaching hours give her more time to devote to her family.
- The school is very well equipped, with brand-new playground equipment.
- She likes the openness and spontaneity of young children; she never knows what they will say or do.

Cathy's short list of dislikes is typical of many preschool teachers:

- She has inadequate benefits. The teachers at her preschool do not have health or medical insurance.
- The close-knit relationships that she forms with her preschool children vanish over the years. Five or ten years later, many do not remember Cathy when they see her on the street.
- The job is physically demanding; she must be able to bounce and jump around with the children.
- She tends to pick up ailments because so many children come to school sick.

The Future

The demand for preschool teachers is increasing far more rapidly than at any other education level. More and more young children are now attending school earlier and earlier because both parents are working. In addition, some states are initiating programs to improve early childhood education—even going so far as to offer universal preschool.

KINDERGARTEN TEACHERS

Kindergarten and elementary school teachers play a vital role in the development of children. What is learned and experienced during the early years can shape children's views of themselves and the world and affect later success or failure in school, work, and life. Kindergarten teachers introduce young children to the world of letters and numbers, open their eyes to the joys of art and music, and help them learn about themselves and the world around them. They are challenged each day to provide interesting, exciting, and motivating ideas that will make young children want to learn. It has been said that all the important things that people need to learn in life are taught in kindergarten. These teachers show children how to share, respect others, tell the truth, and try to do their best at all times. Kindergarten teachers are more than teachers; they are also nurses, referees for fights, supervisors on the playground, temporary mothers or fathers, and, most important, friends to the children. They also happen to be giants in a world of miniature tables, chairs, easels, and playthings.

Preparation for Becoming a Kindergarten Teacher

Kindergarten teachers are considered elementary school teachers and need to meet the same general requirements in order to teach at this level. The exact requirements for becoming an elementary school teacher vary from state to state and province to province.

United States. Today, all states and the District of Columbia require public school teachers to be licensed. Generally, teachers must have a bachelor's degree and have completed an approved teacher training program with a prescribed number of education credits. Some five-year programs exist, and these generally lead to a master's degree as well as teacher certification. Traditional teacher education programs for kindergarten and elementary school teachers include courses designed specifically for those preparing to teach reading, mathematics, science, social science, music, art, and literature. Prospective teachers must also take professional education courses prescribed by the state, such as philosophy of education, psychology of learning, and teaching methods. Teaching skills are acquired through supervised practice teaching in kindergarten or elementary school for about one semester. Because most school districts have continuing education requirements, teachers usually work toward a master's degree.

Many states have reciprocity agreements that make it easier for teachers who are licensed in one state to become licensed in another. In addition, there are emergency certificates for individuals who do not meet all requirements for a certificate when school districts cannot find enough certified personnel to employ.

Also, in most states, elementary teachers have to pass a competency test demonstrating that they have certain basic skills in order to be licensed. In order to show their competency beyond what is required for a license, some teachers may attain professional certification offered by the National Board for Professional Teaching Standards. To become nationally accredited, experienced teachers must prove their aptitude by compiling a portfolio showing their work in the classroom and by passing a written assessment and evaluation of their teaching knowledge. Such certification can give teachers such benefits as higher salaries and reimbursement for continuing education fees.

Canada. Kindergarten and elementary teachers in Canada need to have four years of university education, including a degree and a basic teacher preparation program that includes one year and in some cases two years of professional studies. They also need to hold a provincial teaching certificate issued by the province where they will work. Individual provinces may also require competency tests to be taken.

What Being a Kindergarten Teacher Is Like

In the past, kindergarten classes were typically half-day classes with morning or afternoon sessions. Today, 40 percent of all kindergartens are full-day programs, and teachers typically teach all day. In the first semester of the school year, kindergarten lessons are similar to those taught in preschool, since some of the children have not attended school previously. More focus, however, is placed on skills that the children will need in first grade. Then, in the second semester, kindergarten teachers seriously begin prereading activities, teaching the children the letters of the alphabet and the corresponding sounds. The children prepare for future math instruction by learning shapes and matching, sorting, and counting objects.

Profile of a Kindergarten Teacher

Jackie McVey teaches kindergarten at a private cooperative kindergarten. The parents of her students take turns acting as aides in the classroom, which gives her help from two aides at all times. Not only does she have the opportunity to meet her students' parents, but many of their grandparents also often assist her. A cooperative school is really a family school. Families act as resource people and suggest interesting activities for the class.

As a kindergarten teacher, Jackie is the recipient of a continual flow of affection from the children. She points out that a kindergarten teacher needs to like not only working with children but also dealing with parents. The relationship between parents and teachers at this level is very important in helping young children do well in school.

ELEMENTARY SCHOOL TEACHERS

Teachers at this level usually don't have to handle many of the children's personal needs, unlike both preschool and kindergarten teachers. They are concerned with introducing children to academics as well as guiding the children's emotional, social, physical, and mental development. In the primary grades, one through three, emphasis is on the traditional three Rs. As the children proceed through elementary school, they also are taught history, science, health, and English.

What Being an Elementary School Teacher Is Like

Elementary school teachers spend most of their time in a classroom with a class ranging in size from fifteen to thirty children. The school may have special teachers who will take their students for music, art, physical education, and library. Teachers can use this time for preparing lessons or grading papers. Although most elementary school teachers instruct one class of children in several subjects, in some schools two or more teachers teach as a team and are jointly responsible for a group of students in at least one subject. A small but growing number of teachers instruct multilevel classrooms, which have students at several different learning levels. Elementary school teachers are also expected to supervise their class on the playground and may have additional duties supervising lunchrooms, halls, and bus loading and unloading. Including activities outside of the classroom, many teachers work more than forty hours per week.

Elementary school teachers plan lessons, prepare tests, grade papers, make out report cards, meet with parents, and attend faculty meetings and conferences. They also assign lessons, give tests, hear oral presentations, and oversee special projects. Teachers also have the job of keeping order in their classrooms and diagnosing and correcting learning problems.

Elementary school teachers are required to fill many roles:

- **Disciplinarian.** Making sure that the children follow the set rules
- **Team player.** Working with the other teachers and staff members in their school building
- **Communications expert.** Expressing orally and in writing to parents and other educators how well the children in their class are performing
- **Listener.** Hearing what the students are saying about their problems
- **Referee.** Solving problems that occur between children
- **Motivator.** Encouraging students to want to acquire knowledge
- **Performer.** Grabbing and keeping the attention of the class as they teach each lesson throughout the day
- **Secretary.** Keeping records, filling out forms, and completing reports
- **Jack-of-all-trades.** Having to teach music, art, physical education, and other subjects beyond the basics of their class
- **Lunchroom or playground monitor.** Making sure that everyone is orderly

The Rewards of Being an Elementary School Teacher

Being an elementary school teacher is a good career choice for those who love being around children all day. They will see how their lessons are motivating young children to learn. They will delight in observing how the students in their classrooms are developing and learning during the year they spend with them. Elementary school teachers can take pride in being active participants in teaching children the basic skills they will need throughout their lives.

Profile of a Third-Grade Teacher

Sherry Jagger, a third-grade teacher, has always enjoyed children. Even in her youth, she loved nothing more than spending time with her brother, who was six years her junior. So it was no surprise that when she went to college, she decided to earn a bachelor's in elementary education. Since then, she has gone on to receive her master's degree and has now taught for more than twenty years.

Sherry loves the staff at her school and the friendships she has developed with her fellow teachers. They help her to handle the stresses of her job and also stimulate her with new ideas for her classroom. But she loves teaching most when her students get excited about learning, or when her students who struggle to grasp a concept finally get it. She says, "It excites me." Sherry also takes joy in the sweet, affectionate nature of the children, which makes her job all the more enjoyable. "We have fun together."

Although her students and fellow teachers make her job fun, one of the more discouraging aspects of her job is the widely varying involvement of parents in their children's education. It is difficult for students to excel in the classroom if they are not supported at home, no matter how hard the teacher works or how innovative his or her methods are.

Nevertheless, Sherry strongly feels that the positives of her profession outweigh the negatives. She believes teaching is such a rewarding profession because of the growth that takes place in each child over a school year and beyond. Sherry also says, "Even if you cannot always tell you are making a difference, you realize that ultimately what you do matters."

MIDDLE SCHOOL TEACHERS

Middle school teachers work with children as they are starting to cross the bridge from childhood to adolescence. Rather than teach a wide variety of subjects, these teachers concentrate on teaching within a single subject area such as mathematics, English, science, social studies, reading, art, music, and physical education. Middle school teachers may hold either general elementary or secondary credentials. Preparation for teaching at this level will vary. In general, coursework will include education courses dealing with psychology, tests and measurements, methods of teaching in the particular subject area, and student teaching in that area. In addition, college courses in the subject area will give prospective teachers a solid knowledge of the subject they teach.

Teachers at this grade level can climb the career ladder to become department heads. In this position they are responsible for all the teachers teaching the same general subject, such as English, mathematics, or science. They teach some classes and help the other teachers in the department decide what is to be taught in each class, as well as help them with any problems. At many schools they are also involved in rating teacher performance.

What Being a Middle School Teacher Is Like

Being a middle school teacher is like being both an elementary school and a senior high school teacher. The children receive more guidance than high school students but at the same time have separate teachers for each subject. Teachers at this level will teach five or more classes in their subject area and have a free period during the day to devote to preparation. For each class, they will write lesson plans, make and correct tests, collect homework, and contact parents when necessary. They will be required to perform routine bookkeeping tasks like taking attendance for every class and keeping track of issued textbooks. Besides classroom-oriented work, many middle school teachers are involved in supervising extracurricular activities.

The Rewards of Teaching Middle School

It is a pleasure for middle school teachers to concentrate their teaching efforts on a subject where they have considerable expertise and interest. Furthermore, they have the opportunity to see the children in their classes mature during the school year and to play an important part in helping them grow up.

Profile of a Middle School Teacher

Titus Exum teaches eighth-grade American history. He has a bachelor's degree in elementary education and a master's in school administration and supervision. He holds elementary credentials in Missouri and Alaska. To obtain his present job, Titus had to take the National Teacher Examination.

Titus works as part of a five-person teaching team. Each teacher teaches only one subject; however, they work together to plan assemblies, select guest speakers, arrange field trips, organize field days, and handle other situations involving all of the eighth-grade teachers. He finds that the hardest part of his job is motivating students who are not interested in learning history.

SUBJECT TEACHERS IN ELEMENTARY SCHOOL

Children often leave their elementary school classrooms or have a teacher come to their classrooms to teach them special subjects, such as art, music, and physical education. There are also reading teachers who help children who are having problems learning to read or handling reading in the upper grades. All of these teachers are generally required to have bachelor's degrees in education with special training in their subject area. They will typically hold elementary school credentials with an endorsement in their special area.

Profile of an Elementary School Music Teacher

Teaching music is an excellent way to share a love of music with children. Music teachers do have to make lesson plans, take attendance, and give grades, just like other elementary school teachers. Their work is not easy, as they may see more than five hundred students in a week. In addition, state, district, or provincial guidelines frequently prescribe the curriculum that is to be taught in music classes. Besides normal teaching duties, most music teachers will usually spend time before and after school working with different musical groups and preparing students for special contests and performances.

Julia Scherer has taught music at the same elementary school for more than twenty years. She graduated from college with a bachelor's degree in music education. Like most music teachers, Julia has obtained a master's degree in music and taken additional courses. As an elementary music specialist, Julia teaches general music classes, which feature instruction in vocal music, composers, music reading, instruments of the orchestra, music appreciation, and playing the recorder.

Special Education Teachers

Special education teachers work with the learning disabled, the visually and hearing impaired, and those with mental and physical disabilities. In this job, they work closely with doctors, social workers, psychologists, speech pathologists, occupational and physical therapists, and parents to make sure that each child's individual learning plan is helping the child learn to the best of his or her ability. Special education teachers do not always work in a classroom. They may work at clinics, in resource rooms in schools, or in residential centers. The demand for teachers in this area is very high.

In areas where many children are immigrants and do not have adequate English language skills, teachers are hired as ESL (English as a Second Language) teachers. Their job is to help these children catch up with their classmates. With immigration to the United States increasing, demand for teachers in this area is expected to remain high. Special certification is required to be an ESL teacher. In Canada, teachers who are able to teach French as a second language have their pick of jobs.

Profile of a Special Education Teacher

Lysandra Walker is a teacher of the deaf. Deafness is the hardest sensory loss to overcome, as people learn so much through hearing what others say. Lysandra spends her days bridging the communication gap between her students and teachers and administrators. She interprets for assemblies and classes. She also helps educate the teachers and administrators on the educational needs of the deaf. And above all else, she teaches communications skills to all her students.

SALARY AND FRINGE BENEFITS

What teachers earn in private schools is generally lower than in public schools. The salaries of teachers in public schools are based on the degrees they hold and the number of years they have taught. The median salary for public kindergarten, elementary, and middle school teachers in the United States in 2004 was between $41,400 and $45,920. According to the National Education Association, the highest average salary in the 2005–2006 school year was $58,688 in Connecticut. And the lowest starting salary of $24,108 was paid in North Dakota. In Canadian dollars in 2006, the Canadian Teachers Federation reports the minimum salary for beginning teachers ranged from C$36,920 to C$58,980, while the maximum ranged from C$53,545 to C$83,158. More experienced teachers in Canada who generally have a master's degree earned a minimum salary between C$43,185 and C$64,722, while the maximum range was from C$64,798 to C$94,299. Many teachers work during the summer in the school system or in other jobs, often education related.

Public school teachers have benefits packages that typically include health insurance and life insurance. Furthermore, they have paid sick leave, and most school districts also allow leave days for conducting personal business, handling family emergencies, and jury duty. On certain days during the school year, teachers meet with parents or attend in-service training sessions instead of teaching in the classroom. Teachers frequently join unions, such as the American Federation of Teachers and the National Education Association in the United States. In Canada, teachers belong to provincial unions. These unions bargain with school systems over wages, hours, and the terms and conditions of employment, which may include such issues as class size and pay for supervising extracurricular activities.

Most public school teachers in the United States are obliged to participate in a retirement program under either a state teachers' retirement system or a state public employees' retirement system. Both teacher and school district contribute to retirement programs. Some of these programs offer good retirement benefits. Unfortunately, these benefits cannot be transferred from state to state. In Canada, teachers are required to participate in a retirement plan, and pension credits can be transferred between most provinces.

UNIQUE BENEFITS OF BEING A TEACHER

Certain benefits are unique to the teaching profession. The work year is typically 180 days long. This includes a long summer break (about two months) plus a two-week break in December and a one-week break in the spring. Some school districts now have one-week winter breaks in January. In a number of school districts, teachers now work in year-round schools with breaks between each session and a longer break during the year.

Teachers who have been employed in a school district for a specific number of years and have done their job in a satisfactory manner receive tenure. Tenure is not a guarantee of a job, but it does provide some security. Tenured teachers cannot be fired without just cause and due process. Tenure is usually granted after a probationary period, typically three years.

EMPLOYMENT OUTLOOK

Job opportunities for teachers in the United States will vary from good to excellent, depending on the locality, grade level, and subject taught until the year 2014. The fastest growing states in the West will experience the largest increase in enrollment. Enrollments in the Northeast and Midwest are expected to hold relatively steady or to decline. Teachers who are willing to move or have licenses in more than one subject should have a distinct advantage in finding a job. The job market is especially good for those who are willing to teach in inner cities and rural areas and those with expertise in bilingual education, mathematics, and science.

The job outlook in Canada is dismal for new teachers. Since 2006, teachers qualified to teach junior kindergarten to sixth grade could expect to wait years to find full-time work in some provinces. The best job opportunities are for those willing to teach in rural areas and for those who are French, math, physics, chemistry, and technological studies teachers.

GETTING A HEAD START ON BECOMING A TEACHER

Anyone who is interested in becoming a teacher can get a head start on being successful in this profession by working with children, either as a paid employee or as a volunteer. Being a babysitter is an excellent way to start learning how to deal effectively with children. Jobs in summer camps or at child care centers also give valuable experience, as does volunteer work with youth organizations such as the Boy and Girl Scouts and YMCA groups. Teaching as a career can be explored through teaching at a Sunday school or working as a tutor. In high school, there are cadet teaching programs for those interested in a teaching career.

MORE JOBS IN EDUCATION

The focus of this chapter is on classroom teaching. Some teachers will want to climb the career ladder and become curriculum directors, assistant principals, principals, assistant superintendents, and superintendents. In these jobs, they will still be working for the welfare of children but will no longer be directly involved with their students.

At every school, jobs other than teaching let individuals work closely with children:

School counselor. Elementary school counselors are involved mostly in social and personal counseling. They work with children individually, in small groups, or with entire classes. These counselors also consult and work with parents, teachers, school administrators, school psychologists, school nurses, and social workers. Most school counselors work the traditional nine- to ten-month school year and generally have the same hours as teachers. All states require school counselors to hold state school counseling certification. Some states also require public school counselors to have both counseling and teaching certificates. Depending on the state, a counselor may need two to five years of teaching experience plus a master's degree in counseling in order to get a counseling certificate.

School nurse. Elementary schools may employ school nurses, or one nurse may meet the needs of several schools. School nurses provide a variety of services to students, including giving first-aid treatment for injury and symptoms of illnesses, checking immunization records, performing health screening tests, updating medical records, and teaching in health classes. All school nurses are registered nurses. Some states and provinces require the completion of certain education courses and/or a teacher credential to hold this job.

School secretary. This job involves handling all of the secretarial duties of a school. This will include recording attendance and maintaining students' records. Because the setting for this work is a school, the secretary will also spend time dealing with children's questions and helping with ill and injured children.

School bus driver. Twice a day, school bus drivers in their big yellow buses are working with children. In the morning, they pick the children up at scheduled stops; in the afternoon they return the children home. In addition, they may drive the children on field trips or provide transportation to other schools for special services. Bus drivers must possess the appropriate state or provincial driver's licenses.

Tutor. Tutors provide children with special help in one or more subject areas. They may work in their own homes or go to the children's homes after school, in the evening, or on weekends. Tutors typically charge an hourly rate.

APPLYING FOR A JOB AS A TEACHER

Chapter 13 discusses the details of applying for a job. One step involved in obtaining a job is completing an application. The application shown in Figure 7.1 shows the type of information job seekers must supply to school systems.

Figure 7.1   Application for Teaching Position

115
Educating Children

Date _____

ASSIGNMENT PREFERENCE (1) _____ (2) _____
(Subject or Grade Level)

AREA(S) OF
CERTIFICATION _____
                          Major   Minor

Bachelor's Degree: Major: _____ Minor: _____
                              Semester or Quarter Hours

Master's Degree: Major: _____ Minor: _____
                              Semester or Quarter Hours

Graduate hours completed
beyond Bachelor's or Master's Degree
          Bachelor _____ Master _____

NAME _____
          Last   First   Middle/Maiden

Present Address _____
                              Street

_____ Telephone _____
          City   State   Zip   (include area code)

Permanent Address _____
                              Street

_____ Telephone _____
          City   State   Zip   (include area code)

Date of Birth _____ Place of Birth _____
              (optional)   (optional)

Social Security No. _____ Teacher Retirement No. _____
                                                  (if applicable)

Figure 7.1   Application for Teaching Position (continued)

I EDUCATIONAL DATA

List the high school, colleges, and universities attended or graduated.

	Name of Institution	Location	Dates of Attendance	Degree	Subjects Major/Minor
High School					
College (or) University					
Graduate					
Other					

I am a candidate for the _____ degree to be conferred about _____.

II LICENSE DATA

Applicants should possess a valid teaching certificate or be taking necessary steps to obtain such certification.

Applicant has taken and passed all necessary tests to qualify for certification by the Department of Education.   Yes_____ No_____

Type License	Number	Expiration Date	Subjects or Grades

III REFERENCES

May we have permission to secure your credentials? Yes_____ No_____

Bureau or Agency_____

Address_____

Please list three references, including present and former principals, department heads, or college instructors under whom you have worked. Serious consideration of your application may necessitate communication with one or more of these references. Please indicate a date after which we might make such an inquiry.

Name	Position	Present Address	Telephone Number

IV EXPERIENCE DATA

Total number of contracted years teaching and/or administrative experience _____, subject to verification. Must meet criteria set forth in Article IX (Teaching Experience Credit) of current teacher contract.

School & Location	Dates From To	# of Contract Days per Year	Subject or Grades	Reason for Leaving

STUDENT TEACHING: (if completed within last three years)

School & Location	Dates From To	Subject or Grades	Supervising Teacher's Name and Address

WORK EXPERIENCE OTHER THAN TEACHING: (include military)

Employer & Location	Dates From To	Position or Rank	Reason for Leaving

Coaching Experience of _____

VARSITY COACHING (List in consecutive order beginning with most recent.)

Sport	Girls	Boys	Date From To	Record Won Lost	School District

Figure 7.1 Application for Teaching Position (continued)

OTHER COACHING (List in consecutive order beginning with most recent.)

Sport	Girls	Boys	Date From To	Record Won Lost	School District

Additional Information
List extracurricular activities in which YOU participate—check if willing to direct.

Activities	High School	College	Willing to Direct	Activities	High School	College	Willing to Direct

List positions of responsibility and leadership that YOU have held.

Positions	High School	College	Positions	High School	College

List any special honors YOU have received.

High School	College

Do you play a musical instrument(s)? Yes_____ No_____

Instrument _____ Years Played _____ Instrument _____ Years Played _____

V ADDITIONAL DATA

We are interested in any further information about you that may distinguish your application. This might include travel, honors, publications, advanced study, participation in special programs, extracurricular activities, civic and/or special interests.

_____

_____

_____

_____

_____

_____

_____

_____

_____

Are you now under contract?_____

When are you available for an interview?_____

The information submitted on this application is accurate to the best of my knowledge.
I understand that my application will be retained in current files for a period of one year.

_____   _____

Signature of Applicant   Date

_____

PROCESSING OF APPLICATION (For Office Use Only)

Interviewed by:_____ Date_____

_____

_____

_____

Grade and Step _____

Salary_____

School Assignment_____

Figure 7.1   Application for Teaching Position (continued)

REQUEST FOR BACKGROUND INFORMATION

To All Applicants:

The job for which you are applying with the _____ SCHOOL involves contact with our student population. Please complete the questions below to help us evaluate your suitability to work with these students. All applicants for employment are expected to provide us with this information; you are not being singled out for closer inspection. This insert is part of the Application itself and any misrepresentation or omission of fact may be grounds for disqualification from further consideration or for termination from employment regardless of when the misrepresentation or omission is discovered.

Are you presently the subject of any investigation or other procedure which considers or could lead to your discharge for misconduct by your present employer? Yes ___ No ___. If yes, explain the circumstances on a separate sheet and attach it to this application.

Have you ever resigned from a prior position, similar to the one for which you are applying, under circumstances involving your employer's investigation of your sexual contact with another person, mishandling of funds, or criminal conduct? Yes ___ No ___. If yes, explain the circumstances on a separate sheet and attach it to this application.

*Have you ever been the subject of a charge or investigation by your current or prior employer(s) or a law enforcement agency, implicating you in the sexual abuse of another person? Yes ___ No ___.

*Have you ever pleaded guilty or "no contest" (nolo contendere) to, or been convicted of, any criminal offense? Yes ___ No ___.

If you have answered yes to either of the previous two questions*, please explain, in detail, including the date of the charge, the court action, the offense in question, and the address of the court involved (attach additional pages if necessary):

_____

_____

_____

_____

Conviction of a crime is not an automatic bar to employment. _____ SCHOOL will consider the nature of the offense, the date of the offense, and the relationship between the offense and the position for which you are applying.

AUTHORIZATION AND RELEASE

My signature below constitutes authorization to investigate and examine my employment history and evaluations, as well as my criminal record (if any), in the custody of any private or public employer or any state, local, or federal agency. I further authorize those persons, agencies, or entities that the _____SCHOOL contacts in connection with my employment application to fully provide the _____SCHOOL any information on the matters set forth above. I expressly waive in connection with any request for or provision of such information any claims, including without limitation defamation, emotional distress, invasion of privacy, or interference with contractual relations, that I might otherwise have against the _____ SCHOOL, its agents and officials, or against any provider of such information.

I HAVE READ THIS AUTHORIZATION AND RELEASE OF ALL CLAIMS, AND I EXPRESSLY AGREE TO THE TERMS SET OUT HEREIN.

_____   _____
SIGNATURE   DATE

_____
PLEASE PRINT YOUR NAME

Teachers shape future generations. The more skilled they are, the more they can help children master the complexities of living in today's world. Teachers are constantly challenged to find new and innovative techniques to motivate each child to learn in his or her special way. They also are called on to handle a wide variety of supercharged emotions, from helping a young child adjust to being away from home for the first time to getting a hyperactive child to stay in his or her seat. The job of a teacher is rewarding, challenging, hectic—and never boring.

CHAPTER

8

WORKING WITH CHILDREN IN SPORTS AND RECREATION CAREERS

Indoors and outdoors, sports and recreation activities are very appealing to children. After school, and especially in the summer, they can be a lot of fun. What's more they are very healthy activities, as they discourage a sedentary lifestyle of too much TV, too many video games, and too much time in front of the computer. They also benefit children because they help them make new friends and to feel better about themselves.

Interesting careers await those who wish to help children gain sports skills or enjoy their recreation time. These careers truly present an opportunity to combine avocation and vocation. Karate aficionados can spend their workdays introducing children to the intricacies of this sport. Former basketball players can share their skills with children eager to follow in their footsteps. Camp counselors and directors can help children develop a love of the outdoors. YMCA/YWCA instructors can introduce children to new recreational pursuits. All of these careers let individuals share enjoyable activities with children.

HELPING CHILDREN GAIN SPORTS SKILLS

Team sports leagues for children have taken the place of casual games with neighborhood children. As a result, a great number of children want to improve their skills, and their parents are eager to help them do this. This has opened up a wonderful variety of careers for those who wish to combine a desire to work with children and sports. Of course, few children will ever go on to become sports superstars; however, sports can bring children great enjoyment and satisfaction during their school years and can lead to a lifetime of interest and participation in sports activities. Through sports, children are able to learn many different skills, including ones not just related to sports, such as:

- Handling defeat and victory
- Being part of a team
- Making a contribution to a group effort
- Learning to follow rules
- Learning how to play fair
- Learning how to overcome adversity
- Disciplining their emotions

There are opportunities for careers teaching children such sports activities as swimming, gymnastics, tennis, golf, bowling, ice-skating, bicycling, basketball, baseball, horseback riding, archery, badminton, ice hockey, soccer, scuba diving, fishing, or fencing. Parents are willing to pay for both private and group instruction in sports to help their children gain skills that may lead to participation in a team sport while in school, a possible professional sports career, or simply a lifetime of enjoyment.

WHERE SPORTS JOBS ARE FOUND

Job opportunities are found wherever there is a sufficient population of children. Individuals who want to instruct children in a particular sport work in a number of different settings where the sport can be taught and practiced.

- Nonprofit youth associations provide competitive sports opportunities for children in football, baseball, softball, and soccer.
- Private clubs offer classes at tennis, golf, swimming, and other facilities for children anxious to master a particular sport.

- Parks departments frequently provide instruction in specific sports at facilities designed for those sports.
- Commercial sports centers have the facilities for instruction in one sport, such as bowling, tennis, golf, swimming, or ice-skating.
- Privately owned sports facilities are centers for instruction in such sports as karate, gymnastics, and boxing.

HOW TO BECOME A SPORTS INSTRUCTOR OR COACH

Individuals who are planning to become volunteer coaches can find out about the special training and certification requirements from the National Youth Sports Coaches Association (NYSCA), which is part of the National Alliance for Youth Sports. This organization has a nonprofit certification program that improves the quality and safety of out-of-school sports. Coaches learn first-aid, safety, teaching techniques, the psychology of coaching, sports ethics, and how to make practice sessions interesting and fun. In Canada, the counterpart organization is the Coaching Association of Canada.

For those who are interested in becoming a tennis, golf, swimming, karate, gymnastics, or other sports instructor, certification is highly recommended. Often, one must be at least eighteen years old and certified in cardiopulmonary resuscitation (CPR). There are many certifying organizations specific to the various sports and their training requirements. Participation in a clinic or camp is usually required for certification.

Sports instructors need to have a thorough understanding of the sport they teach. This means knowing the rules of the sport, the techniques needed to gain skill in the sport, and how to teach the sport to children. Many sports have professional associations that offer training programs for instructors. For example, the United States Professional Tennis Association has programs and conferences throughout the year for tennis professionals. And in Canada, Tennis Canada has established an association for all certified instructors, coaches, and club professionals. For swimming instructors, the American and Canadian Red Cross have instructional and certification programs. Sports instructors also need to keep current in what is happening in their individual sports through reading magazines, books, and newsletters and visiting online websites in their sports areas.

WHAT IT TAKES TO BE A SPORTS INSTRUCTOR OR COACH

Besides knowing how to teach and having a genuine desire to work with children, sports instructors and coaches need to have the following aptitudes to be successful in their careers:

- Understanding of how each student learns best
- Ability to communicate with children and their parents
- Ability to share their personal enthusiasm for a sport
- Ability to teach a sport to children with a wide range of abilities, from those who are destined to be champions to those who have limited talents
- Good sense of humor
- Ethics
- High moral standards
- Ability to treat all children fairly
- Ability to handle children's emotional outbursts
- Knowledge of how to build children's self-esteem
- Able to help children develop confidence in their own abilities
- High energy level

THE LIFE OF A SPORTS INSTRUCTOR

Sports instructors and coaches, too, concentrate on teaching sports skills and techniques to children. They generally work the hours that children are not in school, starting work around 3:00 P.M. and working until 9:00 P.M. or even later. Most instructors also have a very full workday each Saturday. In the summer, they are able to concentrate their work in the daytime. However, in sports such as ice-skating and tennis, where limited time is available at facilities, instructors may need to begin work as early as 5:00 A.M. There are opportunities in all sports for part-time as well as full-time positions.

Most sports instructors will give private lessons as well as work with groups. They have to keep track of the progress that each child and group is making and adjust their teaching programs to meet the children's needs. There is some record keeping involved in being a sports instructor, such as recording who attends each session. Unless sports instructors own a facility, they are not involved in the business side of sports instruction.

Being a sports instructor frequently involves more than teaching children a sport. When children enter competitions, sports instructors frequently accompany them to provide additional coaching. In many sports, instructors are responsible for setting up and running competitions and tournaments.

Profile of a Tennis Professional

P. A. Nilhagen was an excellent junior tennis player. He gave his first tennis lesson in Sweden when he was only sixteen and earned six Swedish crowns (about 75 cents). Today, he is the Director of Junior Development for one of the largest tennis programs in the United States.

P.A. was ranked in the top ten of Sweden's junior division at the ages of seventeen and eighteen. He was also a member of the Swedish Junior Davis Cup Team. P.A.'s tennis accomplishments led to a college scholarship in the United States. For four years, he played tennis at Western Kentucky University.

P.A. underwent special schooling and training in order to become a tennis pro. In Sweden, he took training courses to gain certifications. Once in the United States, P.A. became certified by the United States Professional Tennis Association (USPTA). At Western Kentucky University, he received a bachelor's degree in physical education. Today, P.A. continues his tennis education by regularly attending the USPTA's teachers conference held in New York City during the U.S. Open tennis tournament, as well as several other USPTA-sponsored conventions. He subscribes to eight tennis magazines and reads every available tennis book to learn more about the sport. Also, P.A. studies videotapes of televised tennis matches.

P.A.'s first job was as a tennis pro at a very large midwestern tennis facility. After only a few months, he became head pro and shortly thereafter director of the club's junior development program. P.A. is the only coach in the Midwest to remain at one club for more than twenty years. For the greater part of the year, he teaches in the club's indoor facilities. When summer comes, he is outdoors running one of the largest youth tennis programs in the nation.

P.A.'s daily schedule begins at about 5:00 A.M., when he gets up and eats a healthy breakfast. By 7:00 A.M., P.A. has arrived at work, one hour before the first scheduled lesson, to prepare for the day. From then until 5:00 P.M., P.A. is in charge of all on-court activities, which include group lessons, private instruction, and challenge matches. From 5:00 P.M. until 7:00 P.M., he spends time in parent or player meetings.

Even though it is late, P.A.'s day is not over yet. He will probably spend another hour or two talking on the phone with players, to discuss strategies for their next matches. As you can see, a tennis pro does not always work a forty-hour week.

P.A. believes a teacher must do his or her best with every student. He is motivated to find ways to keep lessons from being boring for him or the student he is teaching. P.A. respects his students too much to ever be late for a lesson. He sees himself doing the same job five years from now—only better, because he will have had five more years of experience.

Some of P.A.'s happiest moments on the job are when his students win state, western, or national titles or compete professionally. He especially remembers fondly being at Wimbledon with Todd Witsken and another time when his stepson won the state doubles championship.

P.A.'s advice to prospective teachers or coaches of any sport is to make sure that you love your sport and the people you will be training in that sport. He also suggests finding a role model whom you can emulate. Finally, P.A. believes that sports teachers should stay fit and dress professionally.

Profile of the Owner of a Gymnastics Facility

Terry Spence was a member of the 1968 Olympic gymnastics team but had to leave the squad because of a sprained ankle. Then, while working out for the 1972 Olympic Games, she took a terrible fall. Everyone thought her back was broken. At that moment, Terry, not knowing if she would ever walk again, decided she would teach the sport she loved from a wheelchair if her competitive career was over. Fortunately, Terry's back was not broken, and she was able to end her career in a burst of glory at the 1973 World University Games in Moscow, where she competed against Olympic gold medalist Olga Korbut. There Terry finished the highest, up to that time, for a female gymnast from the United States.

After Terry's competitive gymnastics career was over, she briefly promoted gymnastics for the owner of several gymnastics camps before opening her own studio. When Terry first started her studio, she worked from ten in the morning till one in the afternoon and then returned to the gym at four and stayed until ten at night. Soon, her World of Gymnastics studio had a staff of thirteen and more than five hundred students attending classes for fun and at ten different team competition levels. The studio was open six days a week. On Sundays, the coaches took the students to meets or meets were hosted at her studio. Terry's efficient staff allowed her to trim her teaching hours to between 4:00 P.M. and 10:00 P.M. She was able to reserve the mornings for doing paperwork at home; other staff members taught the sessions for preschoolers.

Terry's happiest moments on the job came when her gymnastics team did well in competition, because she knew she had helped them reach this skill level. On the downside, she found it difficult to deal with parents who expected too much from their children, as well as those who did not believe their children had any potential. Nevertheless, she managed to deal with the parents because she cared so much about teaching children gymnastics.

Terry points out that owning a gym requires one special aptitude: stamina. Owners must have the strength to handle the staff, parents, children, and themselves, along with all the problems running a studio brings.

She feels that the most difficult thing about owning a studio is all the paperwork involved in operating a business, from collecting money and paying rent to buying insurance.

MORE JOBS FOR SPORTS INSTRUCTORS

Individuals should not feel confined to careers in the more traditional sports. While most children have bicycles and enjoy riding them, some children race their bicycles on racing tracks and need instruction to learn more about this sport. Sports instructors teach children archery on indoor and outdoor ranges. Many children are also interested in the martial arts. Name a sport, whether it is scuba diving or snowboarding, and individuals can be found teaching it to children. And the number of sports keeps increasing, and high schools and colleges broaden the spectrum of competitive sports offered at their schools.

EMPLOYMENT OUTLOOK AND EARNINGS

The outlook for jobs as sports instructors and coaches for children is excellent. Job growth is being driven by the large number of children seeking instruction as well as the increased participation of girls in sports. Earnings vary by level of education, certification, and area. Coaches who were stars in their sport or who have coached children who star in a sport will have the highest earnings. Instructors and coaches are paid by the hour, per session, or the number of participants. To get an idea of what a sports instructor might earn, consider the sport of tennis. In the United States, tennis lessons usually range in price from $15 to $75 per hour. However, private lessons at a lush resort can cost more than $100 per hour. Group lessons with four or fewer players range in price from $20 to $80 per hour. Lessons at tennis clubs in Canada often start at C$40 and range to C$60 or more per hour. Semi-private lessons are close to C$60 per hour.

HELPING CHILDREN GAIN RECREATION SKILLS

Recreation refreshes children's minds and bodies. There are some children whose sole concept of recreation is watching television. But recreation is far more than passive watching. It involves playing games, participating in sports, enjoying hobbies, and relaxing. Professionals in the field of recreation introduce children to the vast number of ways they can use their leisure time enjoyably. Their workplace is in parks, playgrounds, gymnasiums, camps, hotels, and even aboard cruise ships and at dude ranches. They work for YMCA/YWCAs, scouting and youth organizations, fraternal organizations, neighborhood clubs, private clubs, tourist businesses, and camps. Most recreation specialists, however, are employed by city and county agencies and work in their park and recreation departments. While the demand for professionals in recreation is increasing, individuals interested in this career need to remember that the number of people employed in recreation is very small compared to those employed as child care workers or teachers.

WHAT IT TAKES TO BE A RECREATION WORKER

Every professional must have certain aptitudes to be effective. Those who want to work with children in the field of recreation need to be far more than "playground babysitters." Some of the aptitudes that recreation professionals should have include the following:

- An ability to motivate children to take part in activities
- An understanding of how to teach skills to children
- An understanding of appropriate activities for children of different ages
- An ability to plan and organize activities
- A genuine love of recreational activities and the ability to transmit that love to children
- An understanding of the kinds of recreational activities children need to round out their lives
- An ability to work effectively with children of different ages
- An ability to work closely with others in developing and executing a program for children

HOW TO BECOME A RECREATION WORKER

Volunteers were once the main source for recreation workers in communities. However, as more and more attention is focused on the recreational needs of both children and adults, competent professionals are required to administer, supervise, and run programs. To meet this need, many colleges have increased the number of courses offered in recreation. These courses are often part of the curriculum in the health, physical education, and recreation departments. An increasing number of full-time recreation professionals now have degrees from two- and four-year college programs. Besides courses in recreation, they take classes in psychology, sociology, communications, and the performing arts. Another important part of their education is on-the-job training in the field for college credit. Even more education is needed by those who want to hold administrative positions in very large recreation and park programs: they are often required to have a master's degree in recreation. While a degree in recreation is helpful in getting a job, it is not essential. Many individuals working in this field have degrees in physical education, health, forestry, education, and even in areas unrelated to recreation. Having work and volunteer experience during the high school or college years does help individuals find careers in recreation. It also helps to be able to teach a skill such as swimming, archery, or canoeing to children.

In the United States, being certified by the National Recreation and Park Association (NRPA) is also a plus for those seeking full-time jobs in recreation.

WHERE THE JOBS IN RECREATION ARE

During the summer most communities have children's outdoor recreation programs in parks. Throughout the year they will have indoor programs in multipurpose centers. Recreation professionals are needed to administer programs at individual parks and centers as well as the entire program of a community. The title of "direct leader" is given to recreation professionals who work closely with children. They are the ones who organize sports contests, bike rodeos, and dramatic productions. They also teach children to swim, play tennis, or dance. Their job frequently includes supervising playground activities and running arts and crafts programs. Full-time leaders need degrees in recreation or related fields. College students can find part-time jobs as direct leaders during the summer and school year. Their salaries are hourly, while full-time leaders' pay is comparable to teachers' pay.

Profile of a YMCA Leader

The entry-level position as a salaried professional at a YMCA/YWCA is as a program director. Program directors are college graduates. Their duties include creating and implementing recreation programs such as adult and youth aquatics, youth sports, parent/child programs, child care, camps, and youth leadership programs.

Thom Martin's career at the YMCA really began at the age of eight months, when he made a big splash in the parent/infant swim program. Since then, the YMCA has been a constant presence in his life, from youth camping and swimming programs to beginning his career at the "Y." While attending high school, Thom served as a YMCA swim instructor, day-camp counselor, lifeguard, movement education instructor, and coach in youth sports. During college, he worked part time as a child care program leader and was also manager of the YMCA pool in the summer. After he graduated, he became the program director at the YMCA where he worked during college. As program director, he handled camping, teen, and parent/child programs. While overseeing the Youth and Government program, he was recognized as Advisor of the Year.

Recognition of his skill as a program director led to Thom's becoming one of the youngest executive directors of a YMCA facility. As executive director, he is responsible for program development as well as regionwide camping programs. Thom explains that YMCA camp is far more than just a fun place for kids to spend time during the summer. He describes it as a place where they can learn and grow, under the guidance of caring counselors, in programs designed especially for them.

Thom says that a YMCA career gives young professionals far more responsibility far sooner than many management jobs. The most rewarding part of his job, however, is the positive impact that many YMCA programs have on children's lives.

What Being a Worker at Summer Camp Is Like

At summer camps, children canoe, swim, ride horseback, toast marshmallows, and build memories that can last a lifetime. And all the professionals who work at the camp, from counselor to director, play a role in helping children learn new skills, gain confidence in their own abilities, and pick up valuable lessons about life. The size of a camp determines the number of employees. The larger a camp is, the more employees it needs to handle the campers, administrative tasks, and other jobs such as cooking, health care, and maintenance. The program staff teaches skills to the children. The counselors supervise groups of children. Division heads oversee several counselors, and the director is responsible for every facet of the camp. Except for the director, all of the staff members are usually just employed for the summer.

Camp counselor. The people who work directly with children at summer camps are the counselors. They share cabins with the children, comfort the homesick, encourage the inexperienced to try new activities, help shy children learn to socialize, teach skills, and generally have fun with the children. Most camps hire college students for counselor positions. They also prefer counselors to have had experience as campers or working with children. In addition, counselors should demonstrate that they have:

- Good judgment
- Initiative and creativity
- Emotional stability
- Good moral character
- Good health and physical stamina
- Good rapport with children

Division head. While the counselors have the direct responsibility of working with the children, someone has to plan and schedule the children's activities, arrange the staff schedule, handle serious problems, and see that the activities are running smoothly. These tasks are handled by division heads, who may have assistants. Division heads are typically in charge of several counselors who are supervising children of a specific age group. Most division heads began as campers and then served as counselors before entering their present positions.

Camp director. At most camps, the only full-time employee is the camp director. The camp director has the ultimate responsibility for every aspect of the functioning of the camp, from seeing that camp rules are enforced to paying all the bills. The director also performs some tasks not listed in the usual job description, such as repairing leaky showerheads, driving the camp bus, or teaching a special class in karate. The director works at the camp during the summer, and in some cases may direct weekend camping sessions throughout the year. When directors are not actively involved in directing camps, they work on organizing and publicizing the next year's program.

What Working for the Boy Scouts of America Is Like

The mission of the Boy Scouts of America is to serve others by helping to instill values in young people, by helping them to achieve their full potential, and, in other ways, by preparing them to make ethical choices over their lifetime. Unlike some other social service organizations, professionals in the Boy Scouts are promoted from within. A bachelor's degree is required to be considered for an entry-level professional position. While work experience is an asset, it is not a prerequisite to working for the Boy Scouts. Most professionals start as district executives, a position responsible for all the scouting activities in a designated geographical area. The district executive recruits, guides, trains, motivates, and inspires the volunteer leaders.

After three years, the district executive can expect to be promoted to a larger district or to start supervising entry-level personnel. The next step, four or five years later, is to a field position managing district executives or to a support program in an area like finance, fund-raising, or directing programs. Through classes at the regional and national levels, professionals receive training that prepares them for advancement in the organization.

Great opportunities exist to have an impact on boys' lives, not only through working in the Scout organization but also through serving as a volunteer. Troop leaders work directly with the boys and can have the satisfaction of being a part of the good this organization does for them.

EMPLOYMENT OUTLOOK

The recreation field offers an unusually large number of part-time and seasonal opportunities. Competition, however, is keen for full-time careers in this area. Opportunities are best for those who have formal training in recreation and experience gained in part-time or seasonal jobs. Overall, growth in jobs in recreation is expected to be comparable to the average of all occupations. Growth can be inhibited at times by the budget constraints local government units face.

THE BENEFITS OF A CAREER IN SPORTS AND RECREATION

One of the best aspects of a career working with children in sports and recreation is simply the opportunity to participate in enjoyable activities with children. While children are not always enthusiastic about school and may not be eager to visit health care professionals, they are generally enthusiastic about sports and recreation activities. Sports instructors have the pleasure of teaching children a sport they truly like, while recreation specialists can enjoy helping children learn ways to use their leisure time.

C H A P T E R

9

KEEPING CHILDREN HEALTHY

Health matters in everything children do. Healthy children are happier and do better work in school. They are eager to play sports and take pleasure in hobbies and other recreational activities. They are better able to enjoy their families and friends. Because children's physical, mental, and social health is so important to their well-being, a great number of careers devoted to keeping children healthy have emerged. Although people tend to think of pediatricians when they think of a children's health career, many others work diligently to ensure that children remain healthy. There are pediatric specialists, nurses and nurse practitioners, pediatric dentists and their assistants, the staff of pediatrics wards and children's hospitals, and the psychiatrists, psychologists, and counselors who help ill or troubled children. A large number of compassionate individuals have chosen these careers because they want to help children, and the demand for these professionals continues to expand. They work in private practice, group practice, hospitals, and clinics.

THE STORY OF PEDIATRIC MEDICINE

Children's illnesses were mentioned in the literature of classical times, and a few books were written about the care of children during the medieval and early modern periods. Hospitals for the care of orphans have existed in Europe since one was built in Florence in 1421. The first hospital for children in the United States did not appear until shortly before the Civil War, when Dr. Abraham Jacobi established one in 1855 in New York City. The first hospital in Canada with the sole mandate of caring for children was the Children's Memorial Hospital in Montreal, which opened its doors in 1904.

In 1880, a pediatrics section was organized within the American Medical Association, and the medical profession recognized at last that children were not simply small adults. Children get diseases that adults rarely contract. Furthermore, children are continually growing, and disturbances in this process cause problems not seen in adults. In addition, the environment greatly affects the health of infants and children.

A great deal of knowledge about the treatment of children emerged in the twentieth century. Many serious diseases that were once considered fatal can now be treated successfully, so the emphasis in pediatrics has shifted toward prevention of illness. Furthermore, it is now recognized that each child has unique needs and special characteristics that must be considered in helping the child develop into a healthy adult.

As more and more knowledge about the health needs of children has been uncovered, a larger number of pediatric specialties has emerged. The number and variety of specialties are a boon for those who want to work with children in health care. Pediatric medical specialties include the following:

Adolescent medicine	Hand surgery
Allergy/pulmonary	Hematology
Audiology	Infant development
Bronchopulmonary dysplasia	Infectious diseases
Cardiology	Neonatology
Cardiovascular surgery	Neurogenetics
Craniofacial anomalies	Neurology
Counseling	Obesity
Dentistry	Oncology/bone marrow
Dermatology	transplant
Diabetes	Ophthalmology
Eating disorders	Orthopedics
Endocrinology	Plastic surgery
Gastroenterology and nutrition	Primary care
Genetic-metabolic	Psychiatry
Genetics	Psychology

Renal
Research
Rheumatology
Speech-language pathology

Spina bifida
Surgery, general
Transplant, cardiopulmonary
Urology

EDUCATION IS A PREREQUISITE FOR HEALTH CARE CAREERS

Plan to go to school to embark on a career in health care. There are vocational school and community college programs for those who wish to be technicians. Some high schools even have programs that will let graduates begin working immediately as a technician after completing school. For many careers as a health care professional, however, a college degree is required. Some even require postgraduate education following college plus additional years of residency training. Furthermore, entry into postgraduate programs is very selective. Successful applicants demonstrate academic excellence and have high scores on graduate school admission tests.

EMPLOYMENT OUTLOOK

The Department of Labor projects a 30.3 percent increase in the number of health care jobs between 2007 and 2014 in the United States. This is a very hot job market. The demand for workers in children's health care is fueled by the growing population of children, and by scientific discoveries and technological innovations that have created new treatments. Health care job opportunities are exploding for both full-time and part-time workers. It is the same story in Canada, where doctor shortages are a top concern. Also, the Canadian Nurses Association predicts a national shortfall of 113,000 nurses by 2013.

PEDIATRICIANS AND PEDIATRIC NURSES

The professionals who concentrate on taking care of the basic health needs of children from birth to adult maturity are pediatricians and pediatric nurses. Besides special training, those choosing a career in this area must have the ability to work well with children and be able to deal effectively with their families. Of course, pediatricians and pediatric nurses are not the only medical professionals associated with the care of children. Physicians in family and general medicine spend approximately one-fourth of their time caring for children. And nurses in hospitals, clinics, and offices also frequently handle the health needs of children.

What Being a Pediatrician Is Like

Today's pediatricians are more likely to work as salaried employees of group medical practices, clinics, or health care networks than in the past. Pediatricians in private practice may work sixty or more hours a week; however, pediatricians who work in groups have more time off because these organizations provide back-up coverage. Most of the work of pediatricians involves treating day-to-day illnesses that are common to children—minor injuries, infectious diseases, and immunizations. While pediatricians spend the majority of their time seeing patients, considerable time is also devoted to dealing with parental concerns over the phone, making regular and emergency visits to hospitals, and keeping records.

Profile of a Pediatrician

Caring for children is as rewarding as ever for Dr. Gustave (Stavie) Kreh, who has been in pediatric practice for more than twenty-five years. Stavie, who adores children, was attracted to pediatrics after working with children in summer camps during high school and college. After graduation from high school, Stavie attended Tulane University in New Orleans, where he majored in sociology and minored in history and chemistry, taking enough science courses to get into medical school.

Stavie attended the Louisiana State School of Medicine in New Orleans after graduating from college. Medical school, he says, teaches the facts and the how-to that every pediatrician needs, but he believes that his liberal arts degree is what gave him the foundation to be an excellent doctor. He wants students who are contemplating becoming doctors to realize that medical school is a tough grind even for students who did well in high school and college. Most medical students are overwhelmed by the tremendous amount of study and memorization that is required their freshman year.

Stavie still remembers the first day of medical school, when he could not even pronounce the words on the professors' mimeographed handouts. Challenged by the difficulty and amount of work that was required of him, he battled back by studying eight to ten hours a day in class and then four or five more hours in the library at night.

"By the end of the intense, four-year medical program," Stavie points out, "you are like a sculpture. You have been chiseled, beaten, sat on, molded, melted down, and refined into a finished product." However, the sculpture was not yet finished: he then had to complete a three-year residency in pediatrics. When he recalls those years, Stavie remembers "horrendous hours, lousy pay, and twenty-four-hour duty every third day." At the same time, it was enjoyable because he was doing what he wanted to be doing.

After completing an army tour, Stavie joined a pediatric practice with four other doctors in Savannah, Georgia. Today, this practice has nine doctors in what is one of the largest pediatric practices in the Southeast, with more than fifty thousand patients. Their office is open 365 days a year at 9:00 A.M. and stays open until every child has been seen, which could be as late as 8:00 P.M. in the winter or as early as 11:00 A.M. in the summer. Stavie designed the group's main ten-thousand-square-foot office building, which has separate waiting rooms with different themes for well babies, sick children, adolescents, and newborns. The group also has two satellite offices.

A typical weekday for Stavie starts at 6:00 A.M., when he checks with his answering service for messages from patients and reports from partners. Then he is off to the two hospitals that the group services, where it usually takes him anywhere from one to two hours to visit his patients and confer with the nurses on each patient's progress or any potential medical problems. Around 9:00 A.M., Stavie arrives at the office, where he sees an average of forty patients a day. On an extremely busy day, he may see up to eighty patients. While seeing so many patients may seem like assembly-line doctoring, Stavie says that most children have illnesses that are easily treated, including headaches, colds, and infections of the ears, respiratory system, and skin. When the occasional emergency arises, however, the pediatrician drops everything and goes to the hospital to take care of the child. Prospective pediatricians need to remember that besides treating sick children, they will also need to spend time attending conferences, monthly pediatric meetings, staff meetings, and hospital committee meetings. They must also oversee finances, computer operations, telephone systems, laboratory equipment, and hiring and scheduling staff.

To be a good pediatrician, Stavie feels, it is necessary to like children, work fast, tolerate night calls from scared parents, empathize with sick children, and have a sixth sense that helps you determine what is wrong when children cannot really tell you.

The happiest moments on the job for Stavie come when he is able to save a child from a life-threatening illness. He also loves when children drop by to see him before they go off to college, just to talk. Stavie's patients are like family to him, and he finds it very rewarding to see them grow physically and emotionally.

Profile of a Pediatric Specialist

Pediatricians and family physicians are the primary caregivers of children. However, they are aided in their work by specialists in the many pediatric health care fields mentioned earlier. Tom Southern, a plastic surgeon, is one of those specialists. During his junior year of medical school, he became totally hooked on a career as a plastic surgeon after seeing the difference a plastic surgeon could make in the life of a burned child. Today, 25 percent of his practice is devoted to the care of children.

A look at Tom's work schedule clearly shows that he is a very busy person. The most difficult part of his job is trying to get done everything that he wants done. Every Monday and Wednesday, Tom is in his office seeing patients continually from nine to five. However, his day does not begin at nine. Before office hours, he visits patients in two hospitals; after office hours, from 5:00 P.M. to 7:00 P.M., he will continue seeing hospital patients. On Tuesday, Thursday, and Friday, Tom is in surgery starting around 8:00 A.M. and continuing until 3:00 P.M. or sometimes 6:00 P.M. Three times a month he is on call in the hospital emergency room, and he also has to take his turn on call in his own private practice. Tom spends his days treating traumas and burns and doing reconstructive and cosmetic surgery. He has treated children as young as one month old.

What Tom likes most about plastic surgery is the variety of surgical procedures that he performs and the different personalities of his patients. However, he dislikes his lack of free time. His advice to anyone who is planning to enter the medical profession, especially plastic surgery, is to be prepared to immerse yourself in your job—but find time for yourself and your family.

Training for Pediatricians

All states and provinces require pediatricians, and all physicians, to be licensed. Licensing requirements include graduation from an accredited medical school (usually four years), completion of a licensing examination, and graduate medical education. Entry into a medical school in the United States requires three years of college or a bachelor's degree; and in Canada, from two to four years of full-time undergraduate courses are required. Students spend the first two years of medical school primarily in laboratories and classrooms. They also learn to take case histories, perform examinations, and recognize symptoms. During the last two years, students work with patients under the supervision of experienced physicians. Following medical school, almost all doctors go directly on to graduate medical education, called a residency, which may last from two to six years—seven in Canada. For those training in a subspecialty such as pediatric cardiology, even more years of residency are required. Doctors seeking board certification in pediatrics take a final examination immediately after residency or after one or two years of practice.

What Being a Pediatric Nurse Is Like

Pediatric nurses are specially trained to provide nursing services to infants, children, and adolescents. They usually work in doctors' offices, hospitals, and clinics. They work closely with but subordinate to physicians in most cases.

Pediatric nurses perform most of the same duties as other nurses, except they work solely with children. They take temperatures and blood pressure and measure height and weight and record all this information in their young patients' medical folders. In the hospital, a pediatric nurse will be assigned to care for several children and will provide such services as taking the patients' vital signs, observing and recording their condition, and giving them medication—the same services adults require. A large part of a pediatric nurse's job is helping to reduce patients' anxiety about treatment.

Pediatric nurses need physical stamina because they spend considerable time walking and standing in their job. They need emotional stability to cope with the pain and suffering of children. Nursing has its hazards, especially in hospitals and clinics where pediatric nurses may care for children with infectious diseases such as hepatitis and AIDS (Acquired Immune Deficiency Syndrome). Nurses must observe rigid guidelines to guard against these and other dangers such as radiation, chemicals used for sterilization of instruments, and anesthetics. In addition, pediatric nurses face possible back injury when moving children, shocks from electrical equipment, and hazards posed by compressed gas.

Profile of a Pediatric Nurse Practitioner

Dan Broekhuizen entered this profession because he loves working with children. He has a bachelor's degree in nursing and a master's degree in nursing with a specialty in pediatrics. Most nurse practitioners have master's degrees, although it is possible to do this work with a bachelor's degree plus additional training. Dan is employed in a pediatric clinic that has three pediatricians. A typical day at work for him involves seeing about twenty-five patients and handling well-baby appointments, physicals, and sick children. Between appointments, Dan has to make phone calls to answer questions from anxious parents about their children's health. According to Dan, pediatric nurse practitioners need physical examination and assessment skills plus the ability to discuss the medical needs of children in terms parents can understand. What he likes most about his job is dealing with children. The least favorite part of his job is dealing with parents.

Levels of Licensed Nurses

There are four levels of licensed nurses. The first is certified nursing assistant, also called a nurse's aide. These individuals aren't actually nurses but work under the direction of nurses. They can be certified for their job with a few weeks of classroom or on-the-job training. The second level is licensed practical nurse. These nurses can get their license in as little time as a year of study. They are the basic nurses in hospitals and work under the direction of registered nurses. The third level of nurses are the registered nurses, who can do a wide variety of medical procedures. The last level is registered nurse with a specialty license. Included in this group are nurse practitioners.

Registered Nurses Training

There are three major educational paths to a registered nursing career in the United States:

1. **Associate's degree in nursing.** These programs are offered by community and junior colleges and take about two to three years to complete.
2. **Diploma.** Diploma programs are taught in hospitals and last about three years. Very few nurses now graduate from these programs.
3. **Bachelor of science degree in nursing.** These degrees are offered by colleges and universities and take from four to five years to complete.

In Canada, registered nurses either complete a three-year diploma program or a four-year degree program, earning a B.N. or B.N.Sc. degree.

To obtain a registered nursing license, all states and provinces require graduation from an accredited nursing school and passing a national licensing examination. Licenses must be periodically renewed, and continuing education is a requirement for renewal in most states and provinces.

Nursing Education Programs

Nursing education includes classroom instruction and supervised training in hospitals and other health facilities. Students take courses in anatomy, physiology, microbiology, chemistry, nutrition, psychology and other behavioral sciences, and nursing. Supervised clinical experience is provided in hospital departments such as pediatrics, psychiatry, and surgery.

Research is essential to find the right educational program in nursing at either the undergraduate or graduate level. Needs and interests must be considered, along with how well established the program's network of nursing contacts is, which will greatly assist the student in finding placement after graduation. The following questions should be asked about any nursing program:

1. Is the program accredited by the National League for Nursing? The National League for Nursing (NLN) of the American Nurses Association

is the official professional accrediting body for programs in nursing in the United States. If a program is not accredited by the NLN, all coursework has to be evaluated before a nurse can continue in a higher nursing education program. In Canada, the accreditation body is the Canadian Association of Schools of Nursing (CASN).

2. Upon graduating from the nursing program, will the school grant a degree in nursing? Many programs grant bachelor's degrees in fields other than nursing; however, graduating from one of these programs will pose difficulties for graduates who are looking for admission to graduate nursing programs where a bachelor's degree in nursing is a prerequisite for admission.

3. What is the image and reputation of the school? Prospective nursing students should talk to graduates of the school and other nurses to find out more about a school as well as get additional information about the program from the NLN or the CASN.

4. What are the credentials of the faculty? Education lies in the hands of a school's faculty. Find out if faculty members are interested in research, have received awards for professional involvement or leadership in the field, and are active in professional organizations (and if so, which ones).

Salary and Fringe Benefits

Pediatricians are generally well paid. In 2007, the median salary of pediatricians in the United States was $110,000, and in Canada it was C$127,700. Those in pediatric specialties can expect even higher incomes. Nurse practitioners working in acute care in hospitals in the United States had median salaries of $73,000, while their counterparts in Canada earned C$70,000. In this same year, registered nurses working in hospitals had a median salary of $52,000 in the United States and C$50,000 in Canada.

Pediatricians in private practice will need to secure their own benefits. Pediatricians and pediatric nurses working in a group practice will participate in a group program; those working at hospitals will have the benefits package offered at their workplace. In addition, nurses are often offered flexible work schedules, child care, educational benefits, bonuses, and other incentives.

CHILDREN'S DENTISTRY

Children need dental care to avoid certain dental problems as adults. The way gums and baby teeth are cared for affects the development of adult teeth. To ensure that their smiles remain perfect, young children go to pediatric dentists, pediatric hygienists, and orthodontists, as well as general practitioners of dentistry.

Employment Outlook

The demand for dentists in the United States is expected to grow about as fast as the average for all occupations through 2014. However, in Canada dental schools are not graduating enough dentists to meet future needs. In both countries, the demand for dental hygienists is exploding. This is largely because hygienists are performing services previously performed by dentists. Unless the number of hygienists increases sharply, opportunities for employment should remain very good in this medical profession.

What Being a Pediatric Dentist Is Like

While dentists may bring to mind images of drilling and filling cavities, dentists who work with children do their best to be seen as individuals who help children have bright healthy smiles. Many work in offices decorated to be appealing to children. They also strive to teach children how to care for their teeth through diet, brushing, flossing, the use of fluorides, and other aspects of dental care.

Although they do have to drill and fill cavities from time to time, pediatric dentists also examine x-rays, place protective plastic sealants on children's teeth, pull teeth, straighten teeth, and repair fractured teeth. They administer anesthetics and write prescriptions for antibiotics. In their work they use a variety of equipment, including x-ray machines, drills, and hand tools such as mouth mirrors, brushes, and scalpels.

Profile of a Pediatric Dentist

In dental school, Donald Bozic found that he was attracted to pediatric dentistry because he was able to communicate well with children and enjoyed treating them. As soon as he graduated from dental school and was licensed to practice dentistry, he started his practice in pediatric dentistry. His training included:

- Four years of college (B.S. in chemistry)
- Four years of dental school
- Two years of specialty training (residency in a children's hospital)

Without his specialty training, Donald could not have limited his practice to children's dentistry.

A typical day begins at 8:00 A.M. and finishes at approximately 5:00 P.M. Donald takes about one hour for lunch. His patients range from very young children to college students. No two patients are alike—not even twins! According to Donald, you need some special skills to be a good pediatric dentist:

- Exceptional patience
- Ability to listen
- Ability to practice excellent dental skills
- Ability to work quickly
- Acceptance that you are working with children

His work environment is definitely child-friendly. It is an open, airy office with a special "monkey room" where hundreds of stuffed toy monkeys cling to the wall. Each young patient can select one of the monkeys to hold while his or her teeth are treated. Donald's happiest moments on the job come when he is able to give children a positive attitude toward dentistry.

Salary and Fringe Benefits

The earnings of dentists in private practice vary according to the number of years in practice, location, and specialty. The median annual earnings in 2007 of dentists in private practice in the United States with one to four years of experience was $96,500, and in Canada it was C$100,000. Those in practice for more than ten years were earning $114,000 in the United States and C$111,728 in Canada. Because they are self-employed, dentists in private practice must provide their own health insurance, life insurance, and retirement benefits.

Training and Other Qualifications for Dentists

All dentists must be licensed to practice in the United States and Canada. To qualify for a license in most states or provinces, candidates must graduate from a dental school accredited by the Commission on Dental Accreditation and/or the Commission on Dental Accreditation of Canada in Canada. They must also pass written and practical examinations. Candidates may fulfill the written part of the state licensing by passing the National Board Dental Examinations. Currently, about seventeen states require pediatric dentists to obtain a specialty license before practicing as a specialist. Requirements include two to four years of graduate education and, in some cases, completion of a special state examination. Most state licenses permit dentists to engage in both general and pediatric practices. Licensing requirements in Canada are governed by the individual provinces.

For admission into most dental schools, a minimum of two years of college pre-dental education (courses in both the sciences and humanities) is required. However, the majority of dental students have at least a bachelor's degree. All dental schools require applicants to take the Dental Admission Test (DAT). When selecting students, the schools consider scores earned on the DAT, the applicant's overall grade point average, science course grades, and information gathered through recommendations and interviews.

Dental school generally lasts four academic years. Studies begin with classroom instruction and laboratory work in basic sciences. Beginning courses in clinical sciences, including laboratory technique courses, also are provided at this time. During the last two years, the student gains practical experience by treating patients, usually in dental clinics under the supervision of licensed dentists. Most dental schools award the degree of doctor of dental surgery (D.D.S.).

Dentists specializing in pediatric dentistry must, of course, like children. Dentistry also requires diagnostic ability, good visual memory, excellent judgment of space and shape, and a high degree of manual dexterity, as well as scientific ability. Dentists who are in private practice also need good business skills.

What Being a Pediatric Dental Hygienist Is Like

Pediatric dental hygienists provide preventive dental care and teach children how to practice good oral hygiene. They show children how to brush and floss their teeth. Depending on the legal restrictions in the state or province where they work, hygienists provide a wide range of services. They examine children's teeth and mouths, recording the presence of diseases or abnormalities. They remove calculus, stain, and plaque from above and below the gum line; apply cavity-preventive agents such as fluorides and pit and fissure sealants; expose and develop dental x-rays; place temporary fillings and periodontal dressings; remove sutures; and polish and recontour amalgam restorations. Dental hygienists use a variety of instruments in the course of their work. They use hand and rotary instruments to clean teeth, x-ray machines to take dental pictures, and models of teeth to explain oral hygiene.

Pediatric dental hygienists work in offices and clinics. On the job they wear safety glasses, surgical masks, and gloves to protect themselves from infectious diseases. They must follow all health safeguards, which include strict adherence to proper radiological procedures, compliance with recommended aseptic technique, and utilization of appropriate protective devices when administering anesthetic gas.

Flexible scheduling is a distinctive part of being a dental hygienist. They may work full time or part time and evenings or on weekends. Dentists frequently hire hygienists to work only two or three days a week.

Profile of a Pediatric Dental Hygienist

Marcia Bozic is an active member of her husband's dental team as a registered dental hygienist. Every two years, she must take twelve hours of classes to keep her license current. Marcia had one year of college before she applied for admission to a dental hygienist program. She then studied in a university dental hygiene program for three years and graduated with a bachelor's degree in public health dental hygiene.

Marcia sees young patients who are scheduled for thirty- to forty-five-minute appointments for cleaning, x-rays, fluoride treatment, and dental education. She likes working with children because it is so much fun to talk with them. And when children walk out of the office, they are wearing rings and carrying stickers and new toothbrushes along with their dental report cards, which describe how well they are doing in brushing their teeth and indicate what treatment has been done and what needs to be done. The dental progress report card can be seen in Figure 9.1.

Figure 9.1   Dental Progress Report Card

151

Keeping
Children Healthy

DENTAL PROGRESS REPORT
Dentistry for Children

Tooth Brushing GRADE (Plaque Score)		
AREAS OF DECAY		
OCCLUSION-Normal		
MALOCCLUSION	a. Skeletal	
	b. Dental (Crowding)	
	c. Minor Orthodontic (Future)	
	d. Major Orthodontic (Future)	
SOFT TISSUE (Gums, Tongue, Lips, etc.)	a. Normal	
	b. Inflamed	

The following treatment was completed today:

1. Examination	
2. Prophylaxis (Cleaning)	
3. Fluoride Treatment (Topical)	
4. Fluoride Treatment (Gel)	
5. Radiographs (X-Rays)	
6. Plaque Removal Instructions	
7. Dental Flossing Instructions	
8. Plaque Disclosing	

Recommendations:

1. Improve (Tooth Brushing)	
2. Plastic Sealants	
3. Restorations (Fillings)	
4. Daily Use of Dental Floss	
5. Disclosing Solution	
6. Daily Use of Fluoride Mouthwash	

Your next checkup appointment should be in:

☐ _____ Months _____

Name _____

Figure 9.1   Dental Progress Report Card (continued)

Grading Scale

THE AREAS MARKED IN RED INDICATE
TEETH TO BE FILLED.

UPPER
TEETH

RIGHT ☐   FRONT ☐   LEFT ☐

LOWER
TEETH

RIGHT ☐   FRONT ☐   LEFT ☐

PRIMARY TEETH

UPPER

NO DECAY ☐

R
I
G
H
T

L
E
F
T

LOWER

The areas marked in Red are those areas of plaque missed when brushing. Your grade depends on the amount of plaque on your teeth.

No Plaque.......................................=3 Points

¹/₃ Plaque ....=2 Points

²/₃ Plaque ....=1 Point

All Covered ....=0 Point

PERMANENT TEETH

UPPER

NO DECAY ☐

R
I
G
H
T

LOWER

Your Grade

A................15–18 Very Good

B................12–14 Good

C................8–11 Average—try harder

D................4–7 Almost failing

F ....0–3 Failing

REMEMBER—A Bright Healthy Smile Depends on YOU!

Salary and Fringe Benefits

Earnings of dental hygienists are affected by where they live, their employment setting, and their education and experience. Dental hygienists who work in private dental offices may be paid on an hourly, daily, salary, or commission basis.

In 2007, the median annual salary for dental hygienists working in family dentistry was $45,000 in the United States and C$45,000 in Canada. Fringe benefits vary substantially by practice setting and may not be available for part-time hygienists. Dental hygienists who work for school systems, public health agencies, the federal government, or state agencies usually have substantial benefits.

Training and Other Qualifications for a Dental Hygienist

Dental hygienists must be licensed by the state or province in which they practice. To qualify for a license, it is essential to graduate from an accredited dental hygiene school and pass both a written and a clinical examination. In the United States and Canada, programs in dental hygiene are accredited by each country's Commission on Dental Accreditation. Although some programs in the states lead to a bachelor's or master's degree or certificate, most grant an associate's degree. Completion of an associate's degree program is sufficient for practice in a private dental office. In Canada, dental hygienists either complete a diploma or a bachelor's degree program.

A high school diploma and college entrance test scores are usually required for admission to a dental hygiene program. Also, some dental hygiene programs prefer applicants who have completed at least one year of college. Requirements will vary from school to school. These schools offer laboratory, clinical, and classroom instruction.

Certain personal qualifications are essential for this profession. Dental hygienists need to work well with others, particularly children, who may be very apprehensive about dentistry. Personal neatness, cleanliness, and good health are additional important qualities hygienists need. Because they use dental instruments with little room for error within children's mouths, they must also have good manual dexterity.

PROFESSIONALS WHO COUNSEL CHILDREN

Some children are so unhappy and distressed or their behavior is so extreme that their parents, friends, and teachers are unable to help them resolve their problems. These children may need special help from a psychiatrist, psychologist, or counselor in order to get their lives back on track and face the future confidently. These professionals are highly trained individuals with years of postgraduate education. Many specialize in the treatment of children and devote most if not all of their practice to children.

Child Psychiatrists

Child psychiatrists deal primarily with children who may need more than advice and a chance to talk things over. Psychologists and counselors cannot prescribe drugs in the treatment of serious problems or disorders; only psychiatrists can. A common example of psychiatric medication is a drug given to treat attention deficit disorder (ADD). Child psychiatrists also use drugs in the treatment of schizophrenia, Tourette's syndrome, depression, sleeping difficulties, and bed-wetting problems.

Child psychiatrists are medical doctors who have had three or more years of training in psychiatry after graduating from medical school. Psychiatrists generally work in private practice, clinics, or hospitals. Child psychiatry is a very small specialty field.

Child Psychologists

Child psychologists provide mental health services to children in schools, private settings, clinics, and hospitals. They help mentally and emotionally disturbed children adjust to life. They also assist children in dealing with stressful situations such as divorce, arrival of a sibling, and death of a family member or friend. Child psychologists counsel children, give diagnostic tests, provide individual, family, and group psychotherapy, and implement behavior modification programs. They may collaborate with doctors and other specialists in developing plans for treatment. Many child psychologists work primarily in elementary and secondary schools. Those in private practice often work evenings and weekends to accommodate the schedules of schoolchildren and their parents. Child psychologists in clinical settings or private practice usually have doctoral degrees, which require from three to five years of graduate work. Psychologists who offer any type of patient care must meet licensing or certification requirements of the state or province in which they are practicing.

Even more so than in other child care occupations, child psychologists must be emotionally stable, mature, and able to deal with people. Sensitivity, compassion, and the ability to inspire children are particularly important for clinical work and counseling. Patience and perseverance are also needed, since the results of psychological treatment often are slow to appear.

Counselors

Like child psychiatrists and psychologists, counselors cannot do therapy with children unless they are licensed by the state or province in which they practice. Those who work in schools in both the United States and Canada often have to have both counseling and teaching licenses and some teaching experience before getting certification. Counselors based outside of school must meet their state or province's licensing requirements.

Many counselors focus their practice on families and children. A children's counselor will help the children of divorcing parents work out their feelings through art, games, role playing, and talking. Or a counselor may help an aggressive boy who is hitting others learn to explore other options for reacting when he is angry at another child. Children's counselors also work with children who are depressed, who don't know how to make friends, who have low self-esteem, who have been sexually or physically abused, and who must learn how to cope with learning disabilities. They may also be called upon to make recommendations in child custody cases. Counselors of children have the goal of giving children the tools and skills to cope with their current problems, so that they have a better chance of becoming healthy adults.

Profile of a Counselor

Bill Shryer's interest in counseling actually began when he was in high school and started working in the psychiatric unit of a hospital. Since then, every career move and every educational degree has helped him become an expert counselor. One of his first degrees, a bachelor's in social work, showed him how social workers deal with personal, family, and community problems. It was, however, his stint in the navy as a neuropsychiatric technician and later work as a psychiatric nurse that gave him a sound medical background. Bill is one counselor who truly understands the role of medication in helping disturbed children and is able to work knowledgeably with the psychiatrists who dispense medicines to many of his patients. While obtaining a master's degree in social work, Bill was fortunate to have as his mentor Judith Wallerstein, who became famous for her study of the effects of divorce on children. Participating in the gathering of data for this study gave him a solid understanding of children's reactions to divorce. To complete preparation for his career, Bill became a Licensed Clinical Social Worker (LCSW) and a Board Certified Diplomate in clinical social work (BCD).

Today, Bill manages three attention deficit disorder clinics and handles the more disruptive behaviors of childhood and adolescence. While part of his day is necessarily devoted to business activities, he typically spends six hours a day in counseling.

Bill's specialty is counseling children; however, he does frequently see children and their parents together. Most patients attend forty-five-minute sessions once a week for six months or less. Then the visits taper down to one or two a month until the problems have been resolved. Bill considers his counseling part of a package. He works closely with pediatricians, social workers, family doctors, psychiatrists, and school districts advocating for children's legal rights under the Individuals with Disabilities Education Act (PL 94-142), the U.S. federal law that provides special education services for all disabled students.

Like truly effective people in every career, Bill is constantly educating himself on new discoveries in his field so he can implement them in his work. He is particularly fascinated by neurobiology and recent evidence that really disruptive behaviors are brain driven, not will driven. His career has become even more satisfying as genetic research now shows that many problems that confront children are based on nature, not nurture.

SPEECH-LANGUAGE PATHOLOGISTS

Speech-language pathology is a career area that deals specifically with improving children's speech. Speech-language pathologists work with children who stutter, lisp, cannot pronounce sounds correctly, or have some other problem with their speech. They assess children's speech difficulties and develop and carry out treatment programs. They work in hospitals, clinics, schools, private practices, or group practices. They are most likely to be employed in a school setting. Within schools, speech-language pathologists may work with just one child or with a small group of children. They will go into classrooms occasionally to help teachers with activities that meet the special needs of children with speech disorders. No matter where they work, part of their job involves counseling parents and instructing them in ways they can help their children. Most states and all provinces require licenses for practicing in this field. To receive certification in either the United States or Canada, a master's degree is required.

Employment Outlook and Earnings

The need for speech-language pathologists is expected to grow about as fast as the average for all occupations through the year 2014 in the United States. Job opportunities within schools will grow as enrollment increases. In Canada, the job outlook for speech-language pathologists is rated as good through 2010. In 2007, the median salary for speech-language pathologists with one to four years of experience was $50,000 in the United States and C$45,000 in Canada.

THE CHILDREN'S HOSPITAL AS A WORKPLACE

One setting where many health care professionals work together to care for children is the children's hospital. These hospitals are equipped to address the entire spectrum of children's health care needs, from preventive care to intensive treatment of injury or illness. One of these hospitals is the Lucile Packard Children's Hospital at Stanford University in Palo Alto, California. The mission of this hospital is to serve all the children of the community who need its special services regardless of their means. The hospital has 650 physicians and 4,750 staff support and volunteer positions, consisting of:

Nursing and patient care support personnel
Professional services (laboratory, pharmacy, radiology, etc.) personnel
Support services (housekeeping, engineering, dietary, etc.) personnel

Administrative and support staff personnel
Physicians
Volunteers

The hospital promotes family-centered care and encourages parents to stay with their children twenty-four hours a day. The staff provides support services for patients and parents, including:

Social services
Interpreters (for more than thirty languages)
Recreation therapy
Family health library
Chaplain
Occupational therapy
Physical therapy
Respiratory care
Nutrition services
Nursing
Hospital school

These descriptions of staff and services at the Lucile Packard Children's Hospital clearly illustrate the range of jobs within the health care profession that deal with children in a hospital setting.

CHILD LIFE SPECIALISTS

Child life specialists primarily care for the emotional, social, and developmental needs of hospitalized children and adolescents. Hospitalized children often experience fear and anxiety related to their illness or injury. Increased levels of stress may also occur when a child is hospitalized. Child life specialists ease the angst of the hospitalized child through developmentally appropriate activities that help children adjust to the hospital environment. They work in major medical centers and children's hospitals. This is a very small and specialized career area. The services of child life specialists include:

1. Playing with the children to minimize their stress and anxiety
2. Teaching hospitalized children and their families about medical procedures
3. Providing distraction and support during medical procedures
4. Developing the emotional, social, physical, and cognitive growth of children during hospitalization
5. Supporting parents and family of hospitalized children; e.g., by answering questions and anticipating needs
6. Supporting hospitalized children and families during times of death and bereavement
7. Performing nonmedical preparation for tests, surgeries, and medical procedures
8. Handling emergency room interventions
9. Providing outpatient consultation with families
10. Using therapeutic medical play with special dolls, stuffed animals, and medical equipment

Training for Becoming a Child Life Specialist

A child life specialist must earn a bachelor's or master's degree. A few universities offer a degree in child life, but most child life specialists earn a degree in a related field such as education, psychology, or child development. Course work must include at least ten classes related to Child Life (i.e. medical terminology, child development, etc.). Child life specialists in both the United States and Canada must complete an internship and pass a certification exam given by the Child Life Council. Those interested in becoming a Director of Child Life must obtain a master's degree. Although not required, it is very helpful to also be fluent in Spanish in the United States and French in Canada. Child life specialists must maintain certification through obtaining professional development hours through continuing education opportunities or attendance at Child Life conferences.

Profile of a Child Life Specialist

Cara Smith is a Certified Child Life Specialist (CCLS) in a major midwestern city. As an undergraduate, she majored in psychology. After graduating from college, Cara enrolled in the Human Development and Family Studies master's program at the University of Missouri. Cara took courses such as death and bereavement, child life theory and practice, and children in the health care setting. Then, she completed an internship for her last semester of study at a local hospital. Upon graduation and after her internship, Cara obtained her first job in the emergency room and child abuse clinic at the same hospital.

The resident physicians with whom Cara works in the emergency room constantly change. Cara finds this to be the most difficult part of her job. Many physicians, while they may have heard of child life specialists, do not always understand their role in the hospital. Cara must advocate for and educate residents on her role in the medical process, especially when working with new physicians.

For Cara, the positives far outweigh the negatives in this job. She is rewarded when patients make progress, and she sees how her work impacts patients and their families. One time in particular, Cara was working with a child on the oncology floor who for many weeks had been struggling with port accesses during chemotherapy. Cara recalls that the child came to her and told her that she wasn't scared of the needle and thanked her for assisting in finding the tools to overcome that fear. It was a significant turning point in her treatment and an eye-opening realization by Cara of the important role a child life specialist can play in children's care.

HEALTH CARE PROFESSIONALS ARE HELD IN HIGH ESTEEM

All health care professionals are held in high esteem for the valued services they provide. And those who care for children are especially appreciated for utilizing their skills to help children recover from illnesses, injuries, and accidents, as well as help them stay healthy. Careers in this area are infinitely satisfying.

CHAPTER 10

ENSURING THE WELFARE OF CHILDREN

In the United States, the first concern for the welfare of children was for the orphans who were often indentured as free labor. It was not, however, until the early 1800s that the first orphanages were established. Then in 1935, the Social Security Act authorized the establishment of child welfare agencies. Since then, child welfare services have increased to cover foster care, child abuse and prevention, family preservation, adoption, and family support services programs. At the end of the nineteenth century in Canada, a consensus developed that the public would have to play a broader role in the care of neglected and abused children. This was due in part to the large number of homeless children on the streets of major cities. Many had been transplanted from Great Britain, others were there because of poverty.

The welfare of the sixty million children in the United States and the six million in Canada today is the major concern of people working in the areas of child welfare and juvenile justice. Unfortunately, there are still children living in homes where they are abused or neglected by their parents. There are also children whose antisocial behavior has brought them in conflict with their families, friends, society, and the law. They are gang members, runaways, truants, and children who commit crimes ranging from misdemeanors to major felonies. People who want to secure better lives for these children can find jobs as social workers, police officers, foster parents, juvenile-court judges, probation officers, juvenile-court referees, and child advocates.

SOCIAL WORK AS A CAREER

Social work is a career for those with a strong desire to help improve children's lives. Originally, it was a career for "do-gooders." Today, it is a large-scale enterprise with more tasks to be undertaken than ever before. Social workers help families cope with problems, provide direct counseling, give concrete information when it is needed, coordinate the services children require, remove children from dangerous situations, and make decisions about the placement of children in foster homes, group homes, and special-care facilities. They also facilitate adoptions.

Most social workers who want to work with children specialize in a single field such as child welfare and family services, children's protective services, or school services. The duties they perform may overlap between fields, and agencies will assign duties differently depending on staff size. The following paragraphs provide brief descriptions of social workers' responsibilities in each field.

Child Welfare and Family Services

Social workers in this field counsel children who have difficulty adjusting socially. For example, if children are having serious problems in school, social workers consult with parents, teachers, and counselors to identify the underlying causes. Some social workers in this field arrange adoptions and help find foster homes for neglected or abandoned children. Also, social workers may work in residential institutions for children.

Children's Protective Services

These social workers investigate reports of child abuse and neglect and intervene when necessary. They may institute legal action to remove victims from homes and place them temporarily in an emergency shelter or with a foster family. Social workers may also be involved in reuniting children with their parents, overseeing the care of children in foster homes, and permanently placing children who have been removed from their parents' care.

School Services

Social workers in this division diagnose students' problems and arrange needed services, counsel children in trouble, and integrate handicapped students into the general school population. They commonly deal with problems concerning misbehavior in class and excessive absences. School-services social workers also advise teachers on how to handle problem students.

Working Conditions and Employment

Social workers are employed in both the private and public sectors. In the private sector, jobs in social work that involve children can be found in social service agencies, community and religious organizations, adoption and foster care agencies, and hospitals. The vast majority of social workers in the United States and Canada, however, are employed by government agencies.

The standard workweek for a social worker is forty hours. These hours, however, can easily extend to evenings and weekends in order to deal with crisis situations and to meet with children and their parents. Furthermore, because of chronic budgetary constraints, some agencies are understaffed, and social workers may find themselves handling huge caseloads.

Being a social worker who deals with children can be a pressure-packed job. There just may not be enough time to handle cases involving children's futures as in-depth as the social worker desires. The work can also be emotionally draining, as social workers try to find the best solutions for children with very serious, even life-threatening problems. At the same time, the work is always satisfying because social workers do improve the lives of many troubled children.

Employment Outlook and Earnings

The employment of social workers is expected to increase faster than the average for all occupations through 2014 in the United States. Leading the way is the employment of school-services social workers in response to rising student enrollment and the emphasis on integrating disabled children into the general school population. Employment in state and local government agencies will also increase because of the increasing need for public welfare family services and child protection services. Many of these services will be contracted out to private agencies that will also hire more social workers. Future social workers need to realize that competition for jobs in cities is much stronger than in rural areas, which often find it difficult to attract and retain qualified staff.

In Canada, job prospects for social workers were only fair in 2007. This is largely because the supply of new entrants to this profession matched the number of job openings. Employment prospects are likely to remain fair until there is increased government funding for social services.

How much one earns as a social worker depends greatly on place of employment. The median annual earnings of elementary and secondary school social workers in 2007 was $40,000 in the United States and C$46,000 in Canada. Those working for nonprofit children's services earned $37,250 and C$42,800, respectively.

Qualifications

The minimum requirement for almost every position as a social worker is a bachelor's degree, and the preferred degree is one in social work. A bachelor's degree in social work (B.S.W.) prepares graduates for direct service positions such as caseworker or group worker. Candidates for B.S.W. degrees take courses in social work practice, social welfare policies, human behavior and the social environment, and social research methods.

In some areas, especially in small communities, it may be possible to secure a job as a social worker with a degree in psychology, sociology, or a related field. However, educational requirements for entry-level positions are becoming more stringent. In many cities, only applicants with master's degrees in social work are being considered for openings.

To obtain supervisory positions in agencies with a large number of social workers, a master's degree in social work (M.S.W.) has almost become a prerequisite for career advancement. An M.S.W. prepares social workers to perform assessments, manage cases, and supervise other social workers. Master's programs usually take two years to complete. It is not essential to have a bachelor's degree in social work to be admitted to a master's program; however, undergraduate courses in psychology, biology, sociology, economics, political science, history, social anthropology, urban studies, and social work are recommended.

Every state and province has licensing, certification, or registration laws regarding the practice of social work and the use of professional titles. Standards for licensing vary by state and province. In the United States, voluntary certification is offered by the National Association of Social Workers (NASW). Social workers with an M.S.W. may be eligible for the Academy of Certified Social Workers (ACSW), the Qualified Clinical Social

Worker (QCSW), or the Diplomate in Social Work (DCSW) credential. Credentials are especially important for social workers in private practice, as some health insurance providers require social workers to have them to be reimbursed. In Canada, registration with a provincial governing body is mandatory in several of the provinces, and membership in a provincial association of social workers is usually required.

One Social Worker's Career Path

Nick Costa is an experienced social worker. His bachelor's degree is in social work, and he is an NASW-certified social worker. Nick's career path clearly demonstrates the competition that exists for jobs in social work. In the metropolitan area where he lives, entry-level social workers at the department of social services must have a master's degree, preferably in social work, or five years of experience in order to work with children. Not having the qualifications for a job at the local department of social services, Nick found a job as a social worker at a private mental health agency that contracted with the county to provide services to the mentally ill. For two years, he worked with mentally ill adults in a program designed to mainstream clients out of mental hospitals and board-and-care facilities. Nick had learned about this job through his counselor at school, which demonstrates the importance of networking as a tool for finding jobs in social work.

Nick's next job was in a rural county close to where he lived. He found out about the opening for a social worker in the Child Protective Services (CPS) department by calling a job hotline. Because competition is intense, Nick prepared very carefully for the interview by talking to social workers in CPS, who described exactly what the job entailed. The preparation paid off, and he was hired to work in a small, overworked, rural CPS department, even though he had no experience in this area. He began by reading case files and received on-the-job training from his supervisor and coworkers. He learned how to investigate reports of child abuse, monitor children's placements in foster homes, and write court reports.

After five years of employment as a social worker in a rural area, Nick applied for a job in the county where he lived, as he now had the requisite experience to be hired. After several years of working in Child Protective Services in this county, he wanted to advance to a position as a supervisor. As a master's degree was required for the position, Nick began investigating where he could obtain a supervisory position without a master's degree.

He found a job through a newspaper advertisement and hopes to advance to a supervisory position in the near future.

Supervisory Positions

Nick's career path as a social worker shows the need to have a master's degree in order to advance to supervisory positions at many social service agencies. Because social workers have such heavy caseloads, it is difficult to combine work and getting a master's degree. The larger an agency is, the greater the opportunity for advancement. The following career ladder shows the progression of positions for social workers in large county agencies:

Director of welfare
Deputy director of welfare
Division manager
Supervisor
Social worker

Supervisors typically oversee the work of six to eight social workers in a particular program, while division managers guide the work of several supervisors. The higher social workers climb on the career ladder, the further they get from working directly with children.

What It Takes to Be a Social Worker

Social workers who deal with children make decisions that directly affect the quality of life many of their young charges will experience in the future. In order to make these extremely important decisions, social workers should be emotionally mature, objective, and sensitive to children and their problems. They must be able to handle responsibility, work independently, and maintain good working relationships with children and their caregivers and with fellow social workers. In addition, social workers need to have the following job-related skills and capacities:

- They must be familiar with the resources available in their community to help children.
- They must be reliable, so the children know that they will visit when they say they will.

- They must model correct behaviors for children.
- They must understand and be able to explain the juvenile court system.
- They must have an excellent memory for names, as they will deal with large numbers of children as well as other professionals who are working with the children.
- They must persuade the children, parents, foster parents, and counselors to act like a team.
- They must promptly return calls.
- They must be able to write clearly so that others can understand what they mean to say.

Specific Social Work Jobs Involving Children

Social-welfare agencies at the county level organize their programs dealing with children in different ways. Social workers may work in just one program, in two programs, or in one large umbrella program. The names of the programs and the exact nature of each will vary throughout the country. Examples of individual programs include the following:

Emergency response. Social workers respond to emergency calls that a child is being abused or neglected. The social workers must decide whether the child needs to be removed from his or her home. Interviews with the child, professionals who know the child (teachers, counselors, doctors), neighbors, and the child's parents are frequently used in the decision-making process. Reports are filed on the disposition of each case.

Reunification. Social workers manage the reunification of children with their families after they have been removed from their parents' care. The children are visited by the social worker in foster homes or in homes of relatives. The children's temporary caregivers are counseled on the care of the children. Meanwhile, social workers also monitor the parents' progress in counseling and parenting classes. Progress reports are written to the courts detailing the reunification status of each family.

Family maintenance. Children who have been made wards of the court are permitted to remain with their families in family maintenance programs. Social workers visit the homes and check with counselors on the progress that is being made to improve the home situation.

Permanency planning. When family reunification programs fail, social workers must develop a case plan and make recommendations to the court for the permanent placement of the child. Some children will be adopted. Others will live with relatives, guardians, or foster parents.

Adoption programs. Social workers investigate the background of the prospective parents and the child to be adopted. Based on their investigations, they make recommendations to the court.

What Being a Social Worker in Child Protective Services Is Like

Social workers who work in child protection are sometimes the highest-paid because the job is so stressful. These professionals have to determine whether an abused child should remain in the home or be removed. This is not an easy decision to make, even after very careful assessment of a situation, because there are so many unknown factors involved. In addition, the decisions social workers make may be monitored by the press.

Profile of a Child Protective Services Social Worker

Mary Doyle is a county social worker in Child Protective Services in a large metropolitan area. Her usual caseload is from twelve to twenty families; she considers fifteen ideal.

Unfortunately, Child Protective Services social workers usually do not begin to work with a family until after the abuse or neglect has taken place and has been reported. Mary attempts to protect children from physical and sexual abuse and neglect. Families are required by law to work with social workers when reports of child abuse have been filed by nurses, doctors, teachers, relatives, neighbors, or others.

Mary does very little counseling. She meets with a family, carefully assesses the situation, and develops a case plan. She tries to get the family to agree on objectives and refers them to whatever services they need, which often include counseling. Then she monitors the situation in order to assess how the family is doing. While the aim is to keep families together, at times Mary must have children removed from their homes to ensure their safety. When this happens, Mary must testify in court.

Reflecting on her career with Child Protective Services, Mary says, "This is a necessary job; someone must do it. You can't say that about all jobs."

As a social worker, she sees people who have been victimized by the system. "It is hard to be a stellar parent when you are impoverished," she says. Mary believes that social workers have a mandate not just to help individuals but also to change society and institutions that may be oppressive.

Profile of an Adoption Services Social Worker

Some children become dependents of the state because parental rights to the children have been terminated by the courts. These high-risk children—abused, abandoned, neglected, or handicapped—are the ones for whom Ed Holt tries to find families. His entire department celebrated when a worker in Ed's unit found a skilled family for an infant who was severely disabled and retarded because of a rare medical condition that required ongoing medical help.

Ed is unit supervisor of adoption services for a county and holds a master's degree in social work. Social workers in his unit have three specific duties. First, they become the child's guardian and make an assessment of the child's adoption needs. After the child is adopted, they make sure things are going well until the adoption is finalized. Second, these social workers study the home to determine what it is like, and they try to match parents and child. Third, they make a genetic search to determine a child's background so that the child and both parents can locate each other, if they wish, after the child is nineteen years old.

Previously, Ed worked in Child Protective Services for twelve years, and positive feedback came from his coworkers rather than the families with whom he worked. Now he is involved in major life events for children and their families. When all the pieces come together and the children and families find permanence that they might not have achieved without his help, Ed's career satisfaction is immense.

POLICE OFFICERS IN YOUTH SERVICES

The primary work of police officers is the safety of a country's cities, towns, and highways. Police officers, however, are also involved in working with young people in trouble—runaways, gang members, abused children, and children suspected of committing crimes. They also work as liaison officers with schools, teaching children about personal and traffic safety and substance abuse. In small communities and rural areas, youth work is often just part of the wide range of a police officer's duties. By contrast, large police departments usually assign officers to youth services departments where they may work in just one area—for example, as a school liaison or in a gang outreach program. Most officers find considerable satisfaction in working with youths. For example, a school liaison officer may see a big downturn in drug activity after presenting a comprehensive drug program at a middle school. Or fights between gangs may diminish because of a youth services officer's efforts to involve gang members in athletic programs.

Employment Outlook and Earnings

The escalation of juvenile crime and the higher incidence of child abuse have led to a greater need for police officers in youth services departments. This demand is increased even more by the current emphasis on school liaison work by police officers. Nevertheless, employment growth in youth services (as well as in other police departments) is tempered by budgetary constraints. The number of job opportunities will vary from year to year and from place to place. Overall, the employment of police officers in the United States is expected to increase about as fast as the average for all occupations through 2014. Job prospects for police officers in Canada are good in 2007 and will continue to be good as long as the number of job openings exceeds the number of job seekers.

The median annual salary for police officers in the United States is $45,000. Total earnings can be much higher because of payments for overtime. Earnings vary by region and the size of the police department. Larger police departments usually pay higher salaries. Furthermore, police officers who work in the West and Northeast earn somewhat higher salaries, while those employed in the South earn somewhat less. In Canada in 2007, the median annual salary for police officers was C$54,500.

Police officers receive common fringe benefits such as paid vacation, sick leave, and medical and life insurance. In addition, most police departments provide officers with special allowances for uniforms. Because police officers are generally covered by liberal pension plans, many in the United States are able to retire at half pay after twenty or twenty-five years of work experience.

Qualifications

Individuals do not apply to become officers in specific police departments, but rather to become police officers. After becoming a police officer, they may then be assigned to youth services or may apply to the department when openings occur. Candidates for police positions in the United States must usually be citizens and at least twenty years of age. In Canada, candidates also need to be citizens and meet the requirements of provincial, municipal, and local police services—all do their own recruiting. Eligibility for appointment as a police officer typically depends on performance in the following areas:

- Competitive written examinations
- Physical examinations, often including tests of vision, strength, and agility
- Oral interviews
- A polygraph test
- Drug testing
- A background check

In some departments, prospective police officers are also given personality tests and may be interviewed by a psychiatrist or a psychologist. Candidates who successfully pass the required tests are then placed on an eligibility list.

Applicants must usually have a high school education. A few police departments accept applicants as recruits who have less than a high school education, particularly if they have worked in a field related to law enforcement. Many departments, however, are now requiring some college training, especially in law enforcement.

Profile of a Youth Services Police Officer

Detective Robin Heinemann is a detective in the juvenile bureau of a large suburban police department. Her childhood dream was to be involved in law enforcement in some way—a dream she began to work on early in her life. By the time she was in eighth grade, she had joined a Law Explorers group, similar to a scout troop. And after high school, she joined a small police department and worked as a reserve officer while she attended college. When Robin was twenty-three, she passed the requisite tests and became an officer in the police department where she currently works. She worked on patrol for four years before applying for and getting her present position in the juvenile bureau, where she works from 8:00 A.M. to 5:00 P.M. Monday through Friday.

In her work at the juvenile bureau, Robin handles a load of fifty to sixty cases at a time. Her cases are generated by a patrol officer at the scene or a citizen making a report to the front desk. She handles cases on a priority basis. Many of the cases involve children who are in middle school. Each case has to be carefully investigated. She often talks to the children involved while they are at school rather than at home. Many of the cases that she handles deal with child abuse. Robin has to establish the facts, corroborate all statements, and put all the facts together to substantiate the allegation. If there is a crime, she writes up a report that goes to the district attorney, who decides on future action based on the evidence Robin presented. In the case of in-home molestation, Robin works with a social worker to take a child from his or her home. Social workers have the authority to place children in protective custody if a police officer signs the appropriate document. Robin follows every case that she handles through to the end. Some cases may only involve a little paperwork, while others may involve extensive investigative interviews. Some will end in the conviction of an adult. Besides handling her caseload, Robin also works as a school liaison officer. In this assignment, she presents programs on safety and substance abuse to schoolchildren.

Robin is well trained for her work through special seminars and in-service training in such subjects as interviews and interrogations and sexual assault and child abuse. In addition, during the course of her police career she has obtained an associate's degree in justice administration, a bachelor's degree in criminal justice administration, and a master's degree in public administration. Other police officers in the youth bureau have similar educational backgrounds.

Because of her interest in children, Robin wants to get more education in child psychology. Her ultimate goal is to obtain a doctorate and become an administrator in the police department.

CAREERS WITHIN THE JUVENILE JUSTICE SYSTEM

The major careers in this area are as juvenile-court judges, juvenile-court referees, caseworkers, and lawyers. Volunteers may serve as court-appointed special advocates for children. Each state or province sets up its own juvenile justice system according to its own laws; therefore, job titles as well as responsibilities will vary. Because juvenile justice is only a small part of the entire judicial system, having a full-time career in this area is usually only possible in cities and large metropolitan areas. Unfortunately, the increase in crimes against juveniles and serious crimes committed by juveniles have led to an increased need for career professionals in juvenile justice.

What Being a Juvenile-Court Judge Is Like

Experience in the practice of law is required, or at least strongly preferred, for most judgeships. The first step, becoming a lawyer, is a difficult and time-consuming undertaking. In nearly every state, prospective lawyers have to pass a bar examination and a separate written ethics examination. And to qualify for the bar examination, it is necessary to have completed at least three years of college and graduated from a law school approved by the American Bar Association or the proper state authorities. To become a lawyer in Canada, a prelaw college or university program must usually be completed and a LL.B. (Bachelor of Laws) degree or a civil law degree obtained. It is also necessary to complete a period of articling, a bar admission course and examination, and obtain a license from a province. The difficulty of becoming a lawyer is heightened because the competition for admission to law school is intense. Furthermore, after individuals have become experienced lawyers, they face stiff competition to become a judge, as so much prestige is associated with the position. Increasing concern about crime and juveniles should spur the demand for judges; on the other hand, tight public funding may slow job growth.

The process of becoming a juvenile-court judge is different in every state. Judges are typically elected or appointed to this position. Judges are appointed in Canada by the federal government and provinces. In large cities and metropolitan areas, many judges concentrate solely on juvenile justice; in rural areas, judges may deal with juvenile cases only one day a month.

Juvenile-court judges have jurisdiction in three areas:

1. Delinquency cases involve juveniles who have committed crimes from shoplifting to major felonies. Certain felonies, such as armed robbery and murder, are often transferred to the adult court system.

2. Dependency cases involve juveniles who have had crimes committed against them, such as abuse or neglect.

3. Status offenses involve acts legally prohibited to juveniles that would not be a crime if committed by an adult. Included in these acts are being a runaway, incorrigible behavior, smoking, drinking, and truancy.

The goal of juvenile justice is rehabilitation. Judges weigh public safety and individual rights in making their decisions regarding the disposition of cases.

Responsibilities of Juvenile-Court Judges

In juvenile court, judges have overwhelming responsibilities in making decisions that directly affect the lives of children. On the one hand, they are handling abuse and neglect cases in which they decide whether children should be removed from or returned to their families, and what services should be offered to those families. On the other hand, they are handling increasingly violent and drug-related crimes committed by children, trying to change delinquent kids' lives while protecting the community.

The role of the juvenile-court judge also includes the following:

- Making sure that all parties appearing before the court receive their legal and constitutional rights
- Ensuring that all the systems involved in bringing cases to court are working fairly and efficiently
- Making sure that there are an adequate number of lawyers, probation officers, police, and social workers to complete the work of the juvenile court
- Keeping abreast of the latest information on such subjects as child abuse, dysfunctional families, and substance abuse
- Exercising a leadership role in the community in determining the needs of at-risk families and providing for the development of services for these families
- Knowing how cases that do not reach the court are resolved
- Monitoring the progress of the child and families to see that the terms of court orders are being followed

- Managing the administration of the juvenile probation department and the juvenile court staff (in some cases)

What Being a Juvenile-Court Referee Is Like

The caseload many juvenile-court judges face is simply so large that assistance is required. Juvenile-court referees act as judges in resolving certain cases involving children. They hold preliminary hearings involving delinquent, abused, and neglected children and make recommending decisions. If the parties involved in the case do not agree with the referee's decision, they can appeal to a judge for review of the case.

Qualifications for being a juvenile-court referee usually include holding a bachelor's degree in the social sciences and having related juvenile or casework experience.

What Being a Juvenile-Court Caseworker Is Like

Caseworkers in juvenile court supervise and counsel youths on probation. They also investigate the backgrounds of delinquent youths to help the judge or referee make the most appropriate disposition of a case. Both juvenile-court caseworkers and caseworker aides may supervise the licensing of foster homes and investigate adoptions. For both positions, related experience plus a bachelor's degree in the social sciences is desirable.

What Being a Children's Advocate Is Like

In describing the Court Appointed Special Advocate (CASA) program, Judge Salvatore T. Mulé, former president of the National Council of Juvenile and Family Court Judges, said, "Abused and neglected children need someone to speak up for them. No one does this more effectively and with more dedication than the CASA volunteer. As a judge, I rely heavily on the CASA's insight and recommendation to the court. CASA does work."

Children can become lost in foster care for different reasons. CASA volunteers in the United States and Canada work to see that children do not fall through the cracks. They are trained volunteers who advise the court about the best interests of children. These volunteers work to ensure that a child's right to a safe, permanent home is acted on by the court in a sensitive and expedient manner. The volunteers conduct investigations and speak with many people—parents, teachers, doctors, neighbors, social workers, foster parents, and especially the child. They review all pertinent records and often become the most knowledgeable person about a child's situation. One of the reasons that the CASA volunteer is so effective is that social workers and attorneys work with many children, while the CASA volunteer is usually only involved with one child at a time. More than fifty thousand people are currently serving as CASA volunteers. Not only is being a volunteer an excellent opportunity to help children, it is also a solid way to gain experience in the juvenile justice system.

THE SATISFACTION OF SAFEGUARDING CHILDREN'S WELFARE

To work in child welfare or juvenile justice is to make a commitment to helping children who are abused, neglected, or caught in a life of antisocial behavior. They are not the "pretty" children seen on television sitcoms, but rather children who have seen the grim side of life. Working in child welfare or juvenile justice is a career in helping the most needy children. The larger dividend is the positive contribution that children whose lives have been turned around will be able to make to society in the future.

CHAPTER 11

INTRODUCING CHILDREN TO THE WORLD OF ARTS AND ENTERTAINMENT

Children's experiences with the arts and entertainment bring joy into their lives. They also broaden their interests and knowledge of the world. A child's education is not complete unless it extends beyond the classroom into new arenas. While schools expose children to the arts, a true appreciation of art, music, dance, and theater is more likely to occur when children see performances or actively study one or more of the arts. Besides participating in and being entertained by different art forms, children seek entertainment from television, books, live performances of children's theater groups, and clowns and puppeteers. Many career options exist for those who wish to share their skills in the arts and entertainment world with children.

CAREERS WITH CHILDREN AND THE ARTS

Those who love the arts can share their intense interest in them with children in a number of careers. Musicians can teach music to the neighborhood children as well as to prodigies at the Juilliard School. Artists can paint or sculpt images of children or teach children these skills. Actors can perform in children's theaters or introduce children to techniques of acting and performing on stage. Instructors are needed to teach dance to children wishing to learn ballet or ballroom dancing. All of these jobs involving children and the arts can be either full-time or part-time positions. While teachers of the arts can find employment at schools, there are also teaching jobs at studios and in homes. Many individuals who teach children the arts are self-employed. Quite frequently, they will also work as musicians, artists, and performers. Their earnings depend on where they live, their experience, and their professional reputations.

What Being a Music Teacher Is Like

Teaching is an excellent way to share a love of music with children—from fledgling musicians in preschool to skilled older children. Each age level offers different challenges and rewards. Prospective music teachers may wish to focus on a particular age group. The setting for teaching music to children can be elementary, middle, and high schools; studios; the children's homes; or the instructors' homes. Information about careers in teaching music can be obtained by contacting the National Association for Music Education (MENC) or provincial registered music teachers' associations. Additional information can be obtained through studying professional journals, including *American Music Teacher, American String Teacher, Music Educators Journal*, and *Choral Journal*.

Employment Outlook and Earnings. Being a private music teacher is an excellent way for a musician to work closely with children. How many students a teacher will have depends on the local demand for music instruction as well as the individual's reputation as a skilled teacher. Since most students are in school during the day, a private teacher's workday does not normally begin until the end of the school day. Fees vary depending on the length of the lesson, the place where it is given, and the area. Fees usually range from $20 to $50 in both the United States and Canada. Those with considerable expertise can earn much higher fees.

Training. Many musicians who become teachers of young children began studying music at an early age themselves. Through their school years, they gained valuable experience playing in formal musical organizations and in small groups with their friends. Musicians need extensive and prolonged training to acquire the necessary skill, knowledge, and ability to interpret and teach music. This training may be obtained through private study with an accomplished musician, in a college or university music program, in a music conservatory, or through practice with a group. For study in an institution, an audition is frequently necessary. Formal courses include music theory, music interpretation, composition, conducting, and instrumental instruction. Many colleges, universities, and music conservatories grant bachelor's or higher degrees in music. Many also grant degrees in music education to qualify graduates for a state certificate to teach music in an elementary or secondary school.

Profile of a Private Music Teacher. Melissa Williams has taught music in elementary school and has worked at a residential treatment center for emotionally disturbed children. Today, she teaches tuba, euphonium, and trombone to about forty students, plays in symphony orchestras in two cities, and does some freelancing at recording studios making music tapes. To get started as a private teacher in a new city, she joined a brass choir and played with a local symphony, where she met many school music teachers who recommended her to students in their classes. In her free time, Melissa practices the tuba, hoping to win an audition to be a regular in a major symphony orchestra. To hone her skills, this accomplished musician takes lessons from an expert player with the Chicago Symphony Orchestra. Her solid educational background in music includes a bachelor's degree in music with a minor in music therapy and a master's degree in performance.

Opportunities in Arts Enrichment Programs

All across the United States and Canada a new career avenue is opening for those who wish to teach music to young children. Group classes now begin for children from birth. These enrichment programs are designed to help young children explore the world of music and movement. They feature such things as singing, expressive movement, musical storytimes, playing simple instruments, and a variety of rhythmic activities. They are taught during the day or evening and may be run by one or two people or a company.

Kindermusik International. In Kindermusik classes, five thousand licensed educators use the Kindermusik curricula in sixty-six countries including the United States and Canada. In these classes, educators lead a group of parents and their children through joyful activities, using music and movement. Parents learn more about their child's particular developmental process, and the shared learning experience creates a unique bond as the child associates learning with fun, musical play. The learning process continues at home, guided by specially designed books, CDs, and games. The organization also provides a license program to teach Kindermusik. On their own, or partnered with community and national organizations and businesses, educators provide classes in such settings as private studios, music studios and stores, community centers, public and private schools, and churches and YMCAs.

FUNdamentals of Music and Movement. This company has programs in Los Angeles and throughout Southern California—serving more than two thousand children. There are age-appropriate enrichment activities, including Parent and Me for infants, Music and Movement for toddlers, and private and group instruction on piano, guitar, strings, and voice. The company's extensive dance program includes ballet, hip-hop, and African. In addition, it offers after-school programs in schools as part of LA's BEST—an education, enrichment, and recreation program serving more than twenty-six thousand students in the Los Angeles Unified School District. In addition, the company offers birthday parties at the center and in children's homes, special events, and a summer camp.

Profile of Arts Enrichment Teachers. Amanda Watkins and Brafo Agindotan both work at FUNdamentals of Music and Movement. For both of them, it is the perfect job at this point in their lives, as they are able to have a career in music—their true passion.

Amanda, who has been singing and playing the guitar since she was five years old, came to California hoping to find a job that would let her pursue her interest in music. She began by teaching piano and guitar to a few private students and working at an arts club as a teacher. The mother of one of her students told her about FUNdamentals—but neglected to tell her how to contact the company before the child quit taking lessons. Fortunately, one day she ran into the woman at a shopping mall. The company was just starting, and Amanda became one of its first employees. Today, she owns a small part of the company. Working full time for FUNdamentals, she conducts music and movement programs both at the center and in preschools. She also gives some private lessons.

Brafo's route to a job also shows the importance of talking to people when you are looking for employment. Both of his parents are musicians, and he definitely wanted to keep music in his life when he looked for a job after high school. He learned about FUNdamentals through his mother and the parent of a student. This was enough information for him. Brafo went in and applied for a job and was hired then and there. Today, he works part time at FUNdamentals as he attends college. Ultimately, he would like to be a music producer and a recording artist. He describes his job at FUNdamentals as a great one because he is able to put smiles on children's faces as they have fun learning about music and movement.

What Being a Dance Teacher Is Like

Children just naturally dance; they can hardly keep their bodies still. Furthermore, they enjoy perfecting their skills through dance classes. Millions of dollars are spent every year for children's dance lessons, from preschoolers learning tap dance and ballet to middle schoolers learning social dancing. Teachers are needed to train all these eager dancers in a variety of settings, such as day care centers, public schools, dance schools, conservatories, studios, and special education programs. Teachers of this art form have the opportunity to actually dance with children as they do their job.

Aptitudes. Dance teachers need to be expert dancers who have teaching skills. The following aptitudes are needed to be a successful dance teacher:

- An anatomical understanding of how the body works
- Ability to relate to children of different ages
- Enjoyment of music
- Ability to choreograph dances for children
- Patience to teach the same step over and over
- Organizational skills needed to break a dance down into parts and then reteach each part until the whole dance has been mastered
- Skills necessary to keep discipline in a class
- A sense of rhythm
- Ability to express ideas, moods, and emotions through dance movements
- Self-confidence

- Creativity
- Ability to work under pressure
- Ambition
- Talent
- Willingness to spend long hours in training and practice
- Good physical endurance
- Leadership ability
- Sincere interest in teaching dance to children and a love of dancing

Besides having dancing skills, dance teachers need to have some business skills. Those who are working at a studio need to know how to negotiate how much they will be paid, while those who have their own studios need to have the skills of successful small-business owners.

Training. The training and educational background needed to teach dance depends on the type of dance an instructor wishes to teach and where he or she wants to teach. Many private dance teachers have trained since early childhood, and their own personal background is the foundation of their teaching. Most of these dancers will continue their own lessons and practice sessions even after they have started to teach dance to others. To teach dance in a public school, it is necessary to have the same degrees and credentials that other teachers have.

Earnings. Dance teachers who work at studios typically are paid by the hour. A beginning teacher can expect to earn between $10 and $30 an hour depending on area and number of students.

What Being a Dance/Movement Therapist Is Like

This career fits within both the arts and medical fields. Dance/movement therapists use the art of dance to improve children's physical and emotional health. The American Dance Therapy Association defines dance/movement therapy as the use of movement as a process that furthers the emotional and physical integration of the individual. To become a dance/movement therapist, it is essential to complete both an undergraduate program with emphasis in psychology and training in a variety of dance forms, followed by professional training at the graduate level and an internship. Dance/

movement therapists also need to be able to perform, choreograph, and teach dance.

The moving body is the dance/movement therapist's medium. The therapist focuses on the communicative, expressive, and adaptive aspects of nonverbal behavior, using these to help clients effect changes in thinking, feelings, physical functioning, and behavior. The method consists of structuring and guiding bodily experience toward an expression of wholeness and self-awareness.

Most dance/movement therapists who are involved with children work in psychiatric hospitals and community health centers. Jobs are also available in hospitals, special schools, rehabilitation centers, developmental centers, and correctional facilities. This field is still relatively new. The American Dance Therapy Association distinguishes between those U.S. and Canadian therapists who are prepared to work within a team or under supervision and those who can work independently. Therapists with the title Dance Therapist Registered (DTR) have a master's degree and are fully qualified to work in a professional treatment system. Therapists with the title Academy of Dance Therapists Registered (ADTR) have met additional requirements and are fully qualified to teach, supervise, and practice privately.

What Being a Children's Artist Is Like

One of the few careers in the arts in which an artist can make a modest profit is painting or sculpting children. This is an extremely small career field. Nevertheless, a few artists become famous for their representations of children and are able to earn an impressive income from their work. Mary Cassatt was one of these artists. One of America's most famous women painters, she is known for her pictures of mothers and children. Only the most successful artists are able to support themselves solely through the sale of their works. Many also work in galleries or in some administrative capacity related to the arts or teach art to support themselves.

CAREERS ENTERTAINING CHILDREN

Adults are definitely not the only group of people who enjoy being entertained. Children are an appreciative audience, too. They thoroughly enjoy being entertained, whether it is by a clown at a children's birthday party, a television program, a costumed figure at one of the Disney parks, or a stage show. Competition for employment as an entertainer is keen. Many entertainers who focus primarily on entertaining children also have other jobs. There are, however, entertainers like The Wiggles and the characters on *Sesame Street* who work full time within this profession.

Profile of a Magician

Steve Hart actually started training to be a magician in fifth grade by practicing with the magician's kit his parents had given him and reading library books on magic tricks. According to Steve, the only schooling that is really helpful in becoming a magician is teaching yourself. First, future magicians study; then they must practice, practice, and practice until they gain skill. Excellent eye-hand coordination is a prerequisite of this profession, and a background in theater can make performances more dramatic. Steve points out that magicians can never stand still; they must always be improving and looking for new and exciting ways to entertain. Steve has invented several tricks, including one in which he makes a two-liter bottle of pop disappear right before an audience's eyes.

Today, Steve uses his skills as a magician to conduct motivational shows for adults. Earlier in his career, Steve gave reading motivation programs in schools. He would show children a book about fishing, and a fish would squirt water on him. When he displayed a book about banking, money popped out. The book on Aladdin breathed smoke. His "Magic of Reading" show for children combined entertainment with the theme of reading. It was a fast-paced, thought-provoking program that encourages children to read and emphasizes the importance of the alphabet, words, and reading. It began with the magical books that he took from his reading treasure chest. With a little more magic carefully applied during his performance, all the books in the chest turned to gold and Steve had sparked the children's interest in reading.

Employment Outlook and Earnings. Magic has become very popular with the advent of the Harry Potter books. Magicians are self-employed and must generate their own business or use an agent. Being a magician is a very small career field. Most magicians are amateurs. It is possible, but difficult, to earn a living as a magician. Starting as a young magician, it is possible to earn from $25 to $50 for a performance. Full-time magicians can earn from $100 at the low range to $850 to $15,000 at the high end. Superstar magicians will earn even more.

Steve strongly advises anyone interested in magic to become a member of the International Brotherhood of Magicians (IBM). Members, who can be as young as twelve, receive a monthly magazine, *Linking Ring*, devoted to the history of magic and the techniques involved in performing tricks. There is even a special section for young magicians. Local chapters of IBM, called "rings," have monthly meetings. There are also international conventions. Steve believes that it is very important for magicians to belong to a fellowship organization where it is possible to mix with other magicians.

Profile of a Clown

Randy Blades is Krackles T. Clown. The *T* stands for *the*. After having his face painted as a clown at a magic convention, he looked in the mirror and decided to become a clown. As Krackles, Randy started making balloon animals for children and then worked a series of shows. Although there are clown schools and even a clown college, Randy is self-taught. In his first year as a clown he made only $10,000. He persevered, however, and today he is scarcely able to keep up with all the programs he is requested to give at child care centers, birthday parties, conventions, and television shows. Plus, he works at several restaurants each week on their family nights. For several years, he and Steve Hart, the magician mentioned earlier, had their own television show, *Wacky Morning Cartoon Club*.

Randy is usually in clown makeup four times a week. When he first started making up his face, he needed over an hour to complete the job. Now it only takes him fifteen minutes. On a typical workday, Randy may perform at 9:00 A.M. and again at 10:15 A.M. at child care centers. Then he may be off to a birthday party at 1:00 P.M. followed by two more child care centers in the afternoon. In the evening, he may perform for adults at a corporate event.

What Being a Puppeteer Is Like

Everyone is familiar with the Muppets; however, puppeteers perform throughout the country in theaters and schools, on local television shows, at malls, and at children's parties. Some colleges even have courses in the basics of puppeteering. Students can learn how to construct puppets and sets, make costumes, and handle the business side of this career. Working as an assistant to an established puppeteer is the best preparation for a career in puppetry. Special skills required in this profession include creativity, manual dexterity, knowledge of what will appeal to a particular audience, and a desire to entertain. Puppeteers may work in such places as Hollywood studios, theme parks, and puppetry centers. Many work for themselves and, like clowns and magicians, puppeteers must spend considerable time soliciting business. The range of annual income for most puppeteers is from $8,000 to $50,000. According to the *Occupational Outlook Quarterly*'s contributing editor puppeteer Paul Mesner, experienced puppeteers who put in the hours can make at least $40,000 a year.

Careers in Television

Children today watch performers on the Disney Channel, public television, and network shows. Many local stations also broadcast shows featuring homegrown television stars interacting on camera with children. This career field is very small and the competition for jobs is intense. Formal training in communications from a college or technical school can he helpful in getting a first job in this field, as can an internship at a local television station.

Careers in Children's Theaters

Across the country, there are children's theater groups that present professional performances for young people. Besides giving children the opportunity to perform on stage and to learn backstage jobs, from creating scenery to costumes, many also offer a wide variety of classes. Depending on the size of the company, there are jobs for a wide range of people interested in sharing their love of the theater with children. For example, the Children's Theatre Company in Minneapolis has a full-time staff that includes a resident acting company, performing apprentices, and other professionals who work with more than three hundred technicians and adults and student actors.

Careers in Children's Book Publishing

The books that children enjoy reading or having read to them are produced by authors, editors, and illustrators. While these professionals do not work directly with children, they do have the opportunity to create books that entertain and educate children. The book publishing industry is centered in New York, Chicago, San Francisco, Toronto, and Vancouver. Although authors and illustrators are typically self-employed and not required to live and work in these cities, editors are usually employed by the book publishing companies located in these areas.

Author. Authors of children's books are creative and imaginative people who are familiar with what appeals to children. Unfortunately, few books are such bestsellers that they produce enough income for the author to live on, and very few authors are able to devote their careers solely to writing children's books. Besides writing the text, some authors also produce the illustrations for their books. Unless authors have contracts to produce books for a publishing house, they must contact, or have their agents contact, a number of publishers and attempt to sell each book they write. This task is much easier after authors have had one or more books published. Once their reputations have been established, writers find it easier to get publishers interested in looking at their latest books or ideas for books. No specific training is required to become an author. Most authors will learn their trade by continually writing.

Illustrator. Most illustrations for children's books are produced by freelance illustrators, although some illustrators work on the staff of book publishing firms. Illustrations play an important role in children's books and must tie in closely to the text. Illustrators must determine the point of view of the author and graphically present it to young readers. Furthermore, illustrators need to have thoroughly developed their technical skills, which they usually have done through training in college, university, and art-school classes. Although illustrators can succeed without formal training, most have bachelor's degrees. Today, there is considerable competition for illustrating jobs from other illustrators as well as desktop publishers and photographers who wish to illustrate books.

Freelance illustrators begin their careers by developing a portfolio of their work to show to editors. Until they develop a set of clients who regularly contract for their work, they may earn very little. Successful illustrators of children's books can earn high incomes and pick and choose the type of work they do.

Editor. The task of a children's book editor is to plan the contents of the books and to supervise their preparation. The editor decides what will appeal to young readers, finds authors to create these materials, and oversees production of the books. Editors hire writers and other employees, plan budgets, and negotiate contracts with freelance authors. They are often helped by assistants who check manuscripts for readability and style and review copy for errors in grammar, punctuation, and spelling.

Most editors have college degrees. They also need to be creative and have the ability to express ideas clearly and logically. The path to becoming an editor usually begins with the position of assistant editor, copyeditor, or production assistant. Because so many people want to be editors, competition is keen for entry-level positions in this field. Serving as an intern in a publishing house or finding a part-time job in publishing is a good stepping stone to a full-time job.

ARTS AND ENTERTAINMENT CAREERS ARE REWARDING

Arts and entertainment careers associated with children are immensely gratifying. They allow individuals to pursue the interests they truly enjoy and share these interests with children. Although this is not a large career area, it is an extremely satisfying one for creative individuals who wish to introduce children to the richness the arts and entertainment can bring to their lives.

12

ADDITIONAL CAREERS WORKING WITH CHILDREN

One in five persons in both the United States and Canada is a child. This means a very large number of children needing a wide variety of services. Some of these services are handled by those in familiar careers, such as child care worker, teacher, and pediatrician. Other well-know careers include those in the areas of health care, child welfare, and juvenile justice. There are also newer careers designed to entertain children or teach them sports and recreational skills. All of these careers have been described earlier in this book. There are also a number of less familiar and new careers in which people can spend their days in close contact with children. A hot new career area is teaching classes to parents and children together. Some careers, like those of research scientist and educational-toy maker, can significantly impact children's lives even though they involve little actual contact with children. Furthermore, new products and companies devoted primarily to children are rapidly being created because of technological innovations. As a result of these changes, there are more careers than ever before in which people can work with or on behalf of children. This chapter describes additional careers associated with the particular needs of children.

A NEW CAREER AREA

Throughout the United States and Canada, parents are joining with their young children in classes and activities that enhance the lives of children.

In them, children are entertained, pick up new skills, and learn to interact with other children while their parents can meet other parents as well as learn such things as new songs and games and parenting skills. Here are some examples of places where job seekers can find employment working with children—most will be in large cities:

- **Play labs.** Stimulate, intrigue, and enhance development of children from birth to three
- **Parent-and-child classes.** Learn dance, music, singing, and movement games
- **Drama classes.** Give early training in dance, drama, music, and art
- **Wellness classes.** Teach parents and babies yoga poses and meditative techniques
- **Cooking classes.** Give children the opportunity to cook and taste the final product
- **Language classes.** Teach children from six months and up another language through games and songs
- **Museum walks.** Acquaint parents and their children with the offerings of museums in their area
- **Mini-gym classes.** Allow children to play on scaled-down gymnastics equipment and run, jump, and climb
- **Postpartum classes.** Teach new mothers such skills as massage and exercise for their babies

WHAT BEING A CHILDREN'S LIBRARIAN IS LIKE

Children's librarians work in large public libraries and school libraries/media centers. They work closely with children or perform tasks that promote children's interest in library materials and reading.

In large public libraries, a separate room is typically devoted to books, periodicals, and media for children. In this room, children's librarians help children find specific materials and make suggestions about books they might like to read. The librarians are also involved in programs with children of different age groups. A library's children's program may have storytelling times for young children, book clubs for older children, and special summer programs for school-age children. The librarians also devote time to creating and maintaining book lists on different topics for the children. A master's degree in library science (M.L.S.) with emphasis on children's services is often required for positions as children's librarians in public libraries. Some master's programs take one year to complete, while others take two years.

School librarians not only help children find the information they need and books they wish to read, they also play an important role in showing children how to use the library. Besides working in the library, they frequently visit classrooms to discuss books, research techniques, and library usage. In addition, school librarians help teachers develop their own book lists and acquire materials for classroom instruction. Many states and provinces require school librarians to be certified as teachers and to have taken courses in library science. To get a job in some schools, it is necessary to have a master's degree in library science or in education with a specialty in library school media or educational media.

Employment Outlook and Earnings

Salaries of librarians vary according to their qualifications and the location of the library. According to the American Library Association, there have been notable increases in the salaries of librarians. The association's 2006 salary survey indicated that the average salary for beginning librarians in public libraries was $40,026 and the average salary for librarians who do not supervise was $45,782. In school libraries, librarians earn salaries similar to those of teachers. In Canada, the median salary for all librarians was C$48,579 in 2007.

The demand for librarians is expected to grow more slowly than other occupations in the United States through 2014. Budgetary constraints in cities and schools are slowing the growth of employment opportunities for librarians. Nevertheless, job opportunities are expected to be very good as a large number of librarians will be retiring. In Canada, the demand for librarians is rated fair; however, the number of job seekers is keeping pace with the number of openings.

WHAT BEING A CHILDREN'S PHOTOGRAPHER IS LIKE

Many photographers specialize in an area involving children, such as children's portraits or school photographs. They may work for a commercial studio or be self-employed. They can be found working in studios, in booths at shopping malls, in children's homes or schools, or at any place that children gather for activities. Skilled photographers capture the essence of the children they are photographing. To do this, they must not only be skilled in the technical aspects of photography but must also have learned how to handle children ranging in age from infant to preteen. Good eyesight, artistic ability, creativity, and manual dexterity are also required.

There is no one best way to become an excellent photographer of children. Individuals considering a career in this field should subscribe to photography magazines and newsletters. Joining camera clubs or working in camera stores can be helpful. Learning on the job is often an effective approach for children's photographers. Attending a college, community college, vocational-technical institute, or a private trade and technical school that offers courses in photography is also useful in becoming a skilled photographer. Basic courses in photography will cover equipment, processes, and techniques. A bachelor's degree, however, will also give fledgling photographers of children a chance to take business courses in case they desire to be self-employed.

Employment Outlook and Earnings

Only average growth is expected in the employment of portrait photographers in the United States and fair growth in Canada. Job growth in both countries is being constrained somewhat by the widespread use of digital photography. In 2007, the median annual earnings for photographers was $30,000 in the United States. In Canada, beginning photographers had median earnings of C$35,000.

WHAT BEING AN EMPLOYEE IN A CHILDREN'S MUSEUM IS LIKE

Many people regard museums as old and dusty places where they can view art, historical, or scientific objects. However, anyone who has ever visited a children's museum knows that they are lively, colorful places with many interactive displays. Children might scamper through caves, ride turn-of-the-century carousels, and watch trains whiz around on a complicated maze of tracks. Unfortunately, children's museums are only found in major metropolitan areas.

Within a children's museum, as within all museums, there are jobs for archivists, curators, administrators, and their assistants. Each individual performs the same tasks that he or she would perform in most other museums, except that the collections in these museums are of items that interest children. The curators might plan and prepare exhibits of turn-of-the-century dolls, live turtles, or the inner workings of the heart. There might be interactive displays in which children can take their blood pressure or investigate how pulleys work. Curators oversee all the collections in the museum as well as acquire new items through purchases, gifts, field exploration, and intermuseum loans. The job of archivists in children's museums is to describe and organize the museum's collections so that individual items can be easily located.

To secure a job as a curator or an archivist, it is just about essential to have a graduate degree, and even then competition is keen as there are so few positions available in these areas. Many individuals have to work as interns, assistants, and even volunteers to get sufficient experience to obtain a job in a museum. Curators will often advance through several positions to become museum directors.

WHAT BEING A YOUTH MINISTER IS LIKE

People who choose careers as youth ministers are seeking to make a difference in children's lives. They also have deep personal faith. Their job consists of planning youth retreats, organizing and managing social functions for young members of their religious groups, and doing some counseling. Their work hours are rarely standard; they regularly work with young people after school, in the evenings, and on weekends.

Most youth ministers find jobs with large congregations. There are no specific requirements for this position; however, most youth ministers have bachelor's degrees in such areas as social work, education, and counseling. They should also have coursework in theology, psychology, and counseling. In some congregations, youth ministers will be priests, rabbis, or ordained ministers. The demand for youth ministers is high in areas that have large populations of young people.

WHAT BEING A SALESPERSON IN A CHILDREN'S RETAIL STORE IS LIKE

Each day millions of dollars are spent by children and their parents on products specifically designed for children. Salespeople who sell children's clothing, toys, sports equipment, books, videos, and learning materials have an opportunity to deal directly with children on many of their sales. They have to stay knowledgeable about the current fads and fancies of young people, which can change overnight. Salespeople also need to know how to communicate effectively with their young customers.

Those who wish to concentrate on selling products to children or products children use can find jobs in small specialty stores as well as the new large stores devoted solely to selling such products as clothing, toys, and furniture for children. There are also jobs in children's departments in large stores.

Employment Outlook and Earnings

It is easy to obtain a job as a salesperson because the turnover rate in these positions is high. There are no formal educational requirements to enter this field. Many people start working in sales as a first job before they even graduate from high school. Employers do want salespeople who enjoy working with children and have the patience and understanding to deal with them effectively. Tired children can be difficult customers.

For many salespeople in the United States and Canada, the starting salary is minimum wage. Overall, in 2007 the median hourly earnings of salespeople in the following cities was: Phoenix—$8.19, Los Angeles—$10.50, Toronto—C$9.00, and Vancouver—C$10.00. Salespeople can work for hourly wages, on commission, or for a combination of hourly wages and commissions. They will not usually receive benefits unless they work full time at large stores. Effective salespeople can become department managers and buyers.

WHAT BEING A CREATOR OF CHILDREN'S PRODUCTS IS LIKE

While individuals who create products for children generally do not work closely with children, they are still pursuing a career that directly benefits children. Children need clothing to wear and toys to play with. Designers of children's clothing will typically work for manufacturers or design lines of clothing for chain stores. Children's toys are constantly being updated, and new toys are created each year. Every one of these toys has been created by a toy designer. Some toy designers own their own companies, while others work for major manufacturers of children's toys. Both the creators of children's clothing and of toys need to understand the psychology of children—how children think and what they want. No formal education is required for these jobs. However, creativity and ingenuity are prerequisites to successful careers in both areas.

WHAT WORKING WITH CHILDREN AND COMPUTERS IS LIKE

With millions of children using computers and the Internet for both recreation and education, brand-new career opportunities are opening up for computer buffs. They can work directly with children, instructing them in the many ways there are to use the computer. Or they may work online answering children's questions about homework and other topics. However, the greatest demand in this area is for individuals who can develop computer programs and websites for children. With the Internet expanding so rapidly, they will find jobs at companies that did not exist just a few years or even months ago or perhaps start their own companies. These jobs require both a knowledge of children and computer expertise. Currently, there is also a need for computer buffs who can create filters to block access to websites unsuitable for children.

STILL MORE JOBS EXIST

The list of jobs that involve children in some way is extremely long. One way to find additional careers that involve working with children is to think of all the places in which children congregate and determine what jobs are associated with these gatherings. For example, in December children stand patiently in line to visit Santa Claus. Thus, holiday part-time jobs exist for would-be Santa Clauses and their helpers. Children also are frequently seen in restaurants that combine food service with an opportunity to play games.

Jobs are available in these restaurants, both as staff and game supervisors. Plus, there is the opportunity to give birthday parties for children and bake birthday cakes for them.

Some jobs associated with children serve children living in other countries. Nightly newscasts often show the plight of children living in third world countries who are impoverished and living without adequate food, clothing, education, shelter, or health care. UNICEF (United Nations Children's Fund) is one organization involved in helping these children. Jobs at organizations like UNICEF are difficult to get because so many highly qualified people apply for them. For example, at UNICEF, minimum employment requirements include a university degree and postgraduate study in a development-related discipline such as nutrition, primary education, public health, or social welfare. Several years of professional work in a developing country is also required, as is written and spoken fluency in English and French, Spanish, or Arabic.

Two programs of the United States government, the Peace Corps and AmeriCorps, provide opportunities to help children. Peace Corps volunteers are sent around the world to help young children learn English and to teach good nutrition to mothers. AmeriCorps is a new national service initiative in which members receive a stipend along with many educational opportunities in exchange for their service. AmeriCorps offers the opportunity to work directly with children in child care centers as well as at CCR&R agencies, where they work with children, parents, and child care providers. In Canada, Voluntary Service Overseas is the country's counterpart to the Peace Corps and is frequently called the Canadian Peace Corps.

In addition, many jobs in science have benefited and continue to benefit children. Jonas Salk made the first polio vaccine, which has nearly eradicated this disease in the United States. Other researchers in laboratories in the United States and Canada are working diligently to conquer serious childhood diseases such as cancer, muscular dystrophy, and Tay-Sachs disease. Any person could become an instant hero upon conquering one of these diseases.

By browsing through newspaper ads and career handbooks and surfing the Internet, it is possible to continually discover new careers involving working with children. No matter what career choice individuals make, working with children can provide immense satisfaction.

CHAPTER

SEARCHING FOR A JOB WORKING WITH CHILDREN

An impressive number of people are needed to raise today's children. Some have a very dramatic impact on their lives—the skilled surgeon who repairs a defective heart, the therapist who inspires an autistic child to speak, the foster parent who provides a haven for an abused child. Others help children learn a skill to enjoy for a lifetime—the pro who teaches tennis, the musician who gives piano lessons, the artist who teaches a child to draw. Still others bring joy to children's lives—the author who writes an award-winning book, the computer guru who creates an exciting game, the clown who makes balloons. So many options exist for everyone who wishes to have a career that involves children in some way. This final chapter looks at where the greatest number of jobs are in this area and describes the best way of finding and getting one of them.

THE BEST AREAS TO FIND JOBS

For those with college degrees, the job pastures are getting greener according to the National Association of Colleges and Employers. What's more, the Bureau of Labor Statistics has identified three specific areas in child care careers that will have significant openings for college graduates until at least 2014. These areas are counseling and social science, with jobs for children's, family, and school social workers; education, namely elementary school teachers; and health care, especially registered nurses and dental hygienists. For those without a college degree, the most promising job area is for child care workers—whether they are caring for children in their own homes, in child care centers, or in the children's homes (nannies, babysitters).

Most of the other career areas discussed in this book offer the same opportunities as the average of all occupations. However, those who are seeking jobs as judges or recreation workers will encounter considerable competition.

THE BEST WAY TO SEARCH FOR A JOB

The perfect job search is the one that results in being hired for the desired job in a minimal amount of time. The right place to look for a job does depend to a certain extent on the type of job. Juvenile judges do not find jobs by searching the want ads, but child care workers can and do find jobs by perusing these pages. Teachers, social workers, and health care professionals also can get job leads through newspaper ads.

Traditionally, the newspaper has been a good starting point for investigating the job market. Now, many people begin their job search on the Internet, where they can find an incredible number of employment opportunities with just a few clicks of a mouse. Beyond sites that list thousands of openings for a wide variety of careers, there are sites for professional organizations, college placement bureaus, private companies, and federal, state, provincial, and local government units. It is also possible to use the Internet to find out average salaries for careers in different parts of the United States and Canada. For many jobs, it is even possible to apply online.

Employment agencies can be effective sources of jobs for certain child care careers. Some agencies actually specialize in finding jobs for teachers, nannies, babysitters, and some health care positions. By visiting one of these agencies, job seekers can obtain a quick overview of the types of jobs available in a community.

College graduates should always investigate the services of their school's career center. These centers usually serve not only recent graduates but all alumni. Career centers will have long lists of job openings with fairly detailed information about each job. Teachers, social workers, and health care professionals can often find jobs by using this resource. Furthermore, career centers often offer information and workshops on getting a job, from how to write a résumé to handling the job interview.

Social workers typically work for public or private agencies, while teachers will work for a school district. A good way to find jobs for these professions is by making direct contact with the organization for which the job seeker wants to work. A phone call or a letter will swiftly provide information about employment opportunities and how to apply for jobs.

Job seekers need to talk about their search. Someone may know a third-grade teacher who is moving across the country, a police department that has the money to hire several new officers in the juvenile bureau, or a private adoption agency that is looking for a part-time social worker. Besides talking to friends and relatives, it is helpful to network with those who are employed in the areas in which job seekers want work. These people often know where job openings are and about positions that may be available in the near future.

CREATING THE RÉSUMÉ THAT WILL ATTRACT ATTENTION

A résumé serves as an individual's introduction to an employer. It is a very important document that can lead to employment interviews. Résumés must clearly present an individual's qualifications in order to be effective. Shelves of books in bookstores purport to tell how to write a winning résumé. And there are many online sites that offer advice on résumé writing as well as provide sample résumés. College career centers, employment agencies, and websites will also have information on how to create résumés that get people hired. Caution: never e-mail a résumé to a prospective employer before sending it to yourself to make sure that it will be received in the format that you want.

Almost every job seeker needs a résumé that details his or her work experience and educational background. Child care centers want to know the background of each potential employee, as do schools, child welfare agencies, and police departments. Parents want to know if babysitters and nannies who will be caring for their children have references available. When employers hire people to work with children, they need to be sure they are employing well-qualified individuals.

Before creating a résumé, job seekers should study sample résumés, especially those of individuals who are employed in the area in which they are looking for a job. Here are some basic hints for writing an effective résumé:

1. Résumés should not have extra-wide margins. A small, difficult-to-read type size should not be used just to fit more information on the résumé.

2. Most résumés should be one page in length. First-time job seekers should not go beyond this limit. More experienced workers should not have more than two pages unless they would be excluding vital education or work experiences.

3. Résumés must be proofread carefully for spelling and grammatical errors. Computer spell-check programs can help in this task. Always have someone check the résumé for errors that may have been overlooked by a computer program or yourself.

4. A heading, work experience section, and education section should always be included on a résumé. If a specific position is sought, the résumé writer should state this in a job objective. Licenses and certificates and professional memberships should only be listed if they pertain to the job that is being sought. Special skills, especially computer skills and knowledge of foreign languages, should be included in résumés. A section should also be used for honors if the honors are of significant distinction. References should not be given on the résumé, but their availability should be stated.

5. A résumé should always be accompanied by a typed cover letter.

The following are actual résumés of job seekers looking for positions (recreation worker, nanny, child care center director, psychologist, and teacher) that involve the care of children.

Timothy N. Davis

465 Clark Drive
Eau Claire, WI 54703
(715) 555-8927
TND@xxx.com

Objective: To work with children in a recreational setting.

Education: University of Minnesota, 2003–2007
                          B.S. in Parks and Recreation

Experience:

6/07–9/07   **Eau Claire Parks Department**, Eau Claire, WI
                          Recreation Worker
                          Organized sports teams and leagues for children
                          under 10. Created programs for each week's
                          sports activities. Taught the correct use of facili-
                          ties and equipment.

6/06–8/06   **Wisconsin Wilderness Camp**, Three Lakes, WI
                          Senior Camp Counselor
                          Provided instruction in boating, swimming, and
                          canoeing. Led three-day canoe trips each session.
                          Supervised eight counselors and planned all camp
                          water activities.

6/05–8/05   Camp Counselor
                          Responsible for daily living and general socializa-
                          tion of 10 boys. Set up camp physical fitness
                          program.

Capabilities: Excellent organizational skills
                          Responsible
                          Able to work well with young people
                          Skilled in working independently

Achievements: Boy Scouts of America, Eagle Scout, 2002
                          Certified in Water Safety and CPR

References: Available upon request.

Georgia Lowell
46 Red Oak Drive
Greenwood, IN 46142
(317) 555-6242
glowell@xxx.com

OBJECTIVE: To provide loving care for children in a safe, creative environment.

EDUCATION: Vincennes University, Vincennes, IN
Child Care Professional Nanny Certification, Fall 2007

Theory course work: Infant-Toddler and Early Childhood Care
Nutrition for Child Care Administration and Educators
Marriage and Family Psychology of Growth and Change
The Nanny as a Professional
Home Management and Family Communications

EXPERIENCE:

10/06–Present *Field Placement*
Vincennes, IN

Work 20 hours a week for a sponsorship family. Provide loving care for a $4^{1}/_{2}$-year-old and a 6-month-old. Duties include supplying basic infant care and stimulation, planning and engaging in age-appropriate activities with preschooler, and performing light housekeeping duties.

9/05–8/06 *Assistant Teacher*, Greenwood Community Preschool
Greenwood, IN

Taught a classroom of children aged $2^{1}/_{2}$ to $3^{1}/_{2}$ years. Responsibilities included providing instruction in age-appropriate activities, implementing daily schedule, assisting children with developmental skills to prepare them for transition to 3-to-6-year-old classrooms, and holding parent-teacher conferences.

6/04–8/05 *Teacher Aide*, Greenwood Community Preschool
Greenwood, IN

Duties included opening the school, teaching in the "practical life" learning center area, watching children who took naps, leading group singing sessions, and performing general housekeeping tasks.

REFERENCES: Available upon request.

Mary N. Young
350 Kelton Avenue • Los Angeles, CA 90024 • (310) 555-1501

Experience:

Center Director

Sunshine Center, Los Angeles, CA
Center Capacity: 112 preschool children,
20 infants, 56 kindergartners, 35 staff

Maintain optimum enrollment by projecting open-ings and filling vacancies. Coordinate children's classrooms by age groupings. Foster open relation-ship with parents and children. Interview, support, evaluate, counsel, and dismiss staff as necessary. Ensure center compliance with state regulations. Assign staff schedule to ensure proper coverage. Maintain staff and children's records. Administer basic first aid and medications as necessary. Write and publish monthly parent and staff newsletter. (8/04–Present)

Center Director

YMCA, Los Angeles, CA

Supervised staff and provided written perfor-mance evaluations. Established emergency proce-dures. Maintained records of children and staff. Responsible for the arrangement, appearance, decor, and learning environment on site. Led staff and Parent Advisory Committee meetings. Turned in monthly reports including cash advance forms and receipts, staff salary projections, staff time sheets, and payroll information. (6/03–8/04)

Teacher

Department of Education, Woodbrook Elemen-tary, San Jose, CA

Serviced children with low or no English profi-ciency with varied whole-language approach. Hands-on sensorial experiences were required to expose children to American culture as well as language. Monitored children once English profi-ciency was established to ensure academic success. (8/02–6/03)

Teacher

Skiles Test Elementary School, San Francisco, CA

Planned and implemented lessons to guide children in development in the following areas: social independence, problem solving, gross and fine motor development, language, music, art, reading, math readiness, and exposure to science. Provided in- depth written evaluations on each child's development in each of these categories quarterly. Met with parents to discuss concerns and achievements biannually in formal conferences. (8/99–6/02)

Education:

University of San Francisco, San Francisco, CA
B.A., Education, 1999

References:

Upon request.

Sharon P. Johnson
1016 Willow Lane
New Haven, OH 57220
(513) 555-2537
johnsonsp@xxx.edu

POSITION DESIRED:	School Psychologist
PERSONAL:	Speak fluent Spanish. Proficient in Word, PowerPoint, and Excel.
EDUCATION:	North Salem University—B.A., Psychology (2004)
	Bellaire University—M.A., Psychology (2005)
	Williamshire University—Ed.S., School Psychology (2007)
CERTIFICATION:	School Psychologist I

WORK EXPERIENCE:

9/06–8/07	**Williamshire University Counseling and Testing Clinic/Department** Position: Graduate Assistant (20 hours/week) Provided career counseling for college students.
6/06–8/06	**Kramer Clinic** Position: Addictions Counselor Counseled teenagers in group sessions in a residential clinic.
6/04–6/06	**Children's Services** Position: Counselor Worked with children in foster care.

OFFICES HELD/ MEMBERSHIPS:	Williamshire University Graduate Council, Student Representative
	Associate of Graduate Counselors at Williamshire University, Vice President
	National Association of School Psychologists, Member
	American Psychological Association, Member
REFERENCES:	Furnished upon request.

Dana Alexander
32 Starmont Drive
Kalamazoo, MI 49002
(616) 555-6812
danaal@xxx.com

CAREER OBJECTIVE

A teaching position in an elementary school classroom for the mildly mentally handicapped.

EDUCATION

Bachelor of Science, December 2007
Major: Elementary Education
Endorsement: Special Education (MIMH)
Ball State University, Muncie, Indiana

Grades:

3.302/4.0 (major), 3.85/4.0 (endorsement),
3.49/4.0 (overall)

Honors:

Kappa Delta Pi (Honor Society in Education)
3/05–present, Dean's List (5 times), EXEL Program

PROFESSIONAL EXPERIENCE

1/07–4/07

Student Teacher, Longfellow Elementary School,
Muncie, Indiana
Taught spelling, reading, math, handwriting,
social studies, and language arts lessons in a
first-grade classroom with 16 students.

WORK EXPERIENCE

6/07–8/07

Secretary, Kelly Services, Indianapolis, Indiana.
Worked at Kraft Foodservice using Word and
performed secretarial duties.

4/07–5/07

Substitute Teacher, Muncie Community Schools,
Muncie, Indiana. Taught grades one through six in
all subject areas to handicapped.

8/04–12/06   Math Grader and Computer Lab Assistant, Ball State University, Muncie, Indiana. Graded math exams, loaded computers, and helped students having problems with educational software.

ACTIVITIES

Volunteered to help an autistic child using the Sun-Rise program, 1/04–5/04.

REFERENCES

Available upon request.

CREATING OUTSTANDING COVER LETTERS

An outstanding cover letter compels the recipient to look attentively at an individual's résumé, while a poor cover letter may discourage the recipient from even looking at the résumé at all. The purpose of the cover letter is to introduce the job applicant, explain why the résumé has been sent, and request an interview. The following information should usually be included in the cover letter:

1. The writer's name and address, unless a personal letterhead is used
2. The date
3. The name and title of the person to whom the résumé is being sent and the organization name and address
4. The salutation: "Dear Mr. Jones," "Ms. Smith," "Dr. Johnson," or "To Whom It May Concern"
5. An opening paragraph explaining why the applicant is writing, and stating the position being sought
6. One or more paragraphs pointing out why the applicant would like to work for the organization and the qualifications the applicant has
7. A final paragraph requesting an interview
8. The closing: "Sincerely," or "Yours truly," followed by the applicant's signature and name typed under the signature

Cover letters should not be more than one page in length. The tone of the letter should be formal and businesslike. The cover letters on the next pages were written by first-time job seekers.

MARGARET JONES
368 BIRCH DRIVE
KENOSHA, WI 53143
(414) 555-5604
margaretjones@xxx.net

April 17, 20__

Mr. Clark Adams, Principal
Clay Elementary School
3500 Main Street
Naperville, IL 60565

Dear Mr. Adams:

I will be graduating from the University of Wisconsin in May. I am seeking an elementary school teaching position in second grade.

My education from the University of Wisconsin has exposed me to the latest developments in the teaching profession. It has also given me the opportunity to participate in different classroom situations. I plan to continue my professional growth in the future by pursuing a master's degree in education.

Enclosed, you will find my résumé. A complete credentials file is available upon request through the University of Wisconsin: Educational Placement Office, 4600 Sunset Avenue, Madison, Wisconsin 53709, (608) 555-3000.

I would like to request an interview with the Clay School Corporation at this time. I may be contacted at the above address or phone number. Could you please send me informational literature on your school corporation? Thank you.

Sincerely,

Margaret Jones

Margaret Jones

Enclosure

MARK G. YOUNG

26430 HUDSON LANE
DOVER, DE 19901
(302) 555-8947
mgyoung@xxx.com

June 12, 20__

Mr. Peter Wiggins, Executive Director
Dover Department of Social Services
965 Park Avenue
Dover, DE 19901

Dear Mr. Wiggins:

I am writing to inquire whether the Dover Department of Social Services has an opening for a social worker in your Children's Protective Services program. Having a bachelor's degree in social work and experience working with children at a women's shelter for the past two summers, I feel that I am well qualified to be a social worker.

My volunteer experience as a Big Brother has taught me how to relate effectively with abused children. In addition, my 400 hours of supervised field experience has been in a Children's Protective Services program. This has acquainted me with the services abused children need.

I would appreciate the opportunity to discuss my qualifications and abilities with you at length in an interview.

Sincerely,

Mark G. Young

Mark G. Young

Janet Lynn Gomez
3800 Alvarado Boulevard
San Antonio, TX 78243
(210) 555-4335
jlnngomez@xxx.com

May 9, 20__

Dr. Colleen LeRoy
Children's Dental Clinic
5420 Ramona Avenue
Austin, TX 78501

Dear Dr. LeRoy:

I am writing in response to your advertisement in the Sunday edition of the *Austin American-Statesman* for a dental hygienist. The position greatly interests me, as I am especially interested in working with children.

I have just received my Texas dental hygienist license and am eager to begin my career. Furthermore, I have completed two years of college at Concordia University.

A résumé is enclosed that reflects my academic and work experience. I am confident that my background would make me an asset to the clinic.

I look forward to hearing from you soon. Thank you for your consideration.

Sincerely,

Janet Lynn Gomez

Janet Lynn Gomez

Enclosure

340 Bristol Drive
Richmond, VA 23285
(804) 555-8756
gstanton@aol.com

March 10, 20__

Harvey Gifford
Valley Tennis Club
20009 First Street NW
Santa Clara, CA 95054

Dear Mr. Gifford:

Roger Adams of the United States Tennis Association referred me to you because of your club's need for a professional to establish a junior program. I would be very interested in discussing this position with you.

I will be graduating from the University of San Francisco in May 20__ with a major in recreation. Besides working for the past two summers with the junior tennis program of the Santa Clara County Parks Department, I was a ranked junior player in California and a member of my college tennis team.

My résumé is enclosed for your review. I will call you on Friday to set up an appointment to talk about how I might be useful in setting up Valley Tennis Club's new youth program. I look forward to meeting with you.

Sincerely,

George Stanton

George Stanton

Enclosure

DOING ONE'S BEST AT AN INTERVIEW

Cover letters and résumés are very important components of getting a job; however, the interview is the deal maker or breaker. The more prepared an applicant is for an interview, the higher the chance of securing a job. In preparing for an interview, applicants must determine how they want to describe themselves to the interviewer. At the same time, they need to consider what questions they have for the interviewer about the organization, because in every interview, the interviewer eventually asks, "Do you have any questions?" The best interviews are truly information sharing sessions.

Job applicants need to be as diligent in their preparation for an interview as the president is before a press conference. The best preparation for prospective interviewees is to actually say aloud several times exactly what they would like the interviewer to know about themselves. They should also prepare answers to the following questions, which are frequently asked at interviews.

1. Why should this organization hire you?
2. What are your greatest strengths and weaknesses?
3. In what ways do you think you will make a contribution to this organization?
4. Why did you choose this career?
5. What are your long-range career objectives?
6. What two or three accomplishments in your life have given you the greatest satisfaction? Why?
7. Why did you decide to apply for a job with this organization?
8. How would you describe yourself?
9. How do you plan to achieve your career goals?
10. What motivates you to put forth your greatest effort?

Some job seekers find it helpful to hold practice interview sessions in which friends or family members ask them possible interview questions. Practicing answers to questions ahead of time makes answering similar questions much easier at the time of the interview.

Before any interview, job seekers must always find out as much as they can about the organization they are interviewing with and what their job duties in the position would be. For example, an applicant for the job of school psychologist needs to know if his or her position will involve primarily testing or counseling or some combination of these two responsibilities. Information about large organizations can be obtained by reading about them or visiting their websites. Some organizations have newsletters, which give applicants an idea of the feel and the tone of the organization. However, the information that most child care workers need is more likely to come from individuals actually working at the organization or the actual job for which the person is applying.

Once the applicant has solidly prepared what he or she would like to say at the interview, it is time to consider some practical details. An outfit for the interview should be carefully chosen. It should be in keeping with company standards for the position being sought. Also, the applicant should become familiar with the route to the interview site in order to arrive early.

THE ACTUAL INTERVIEW

At large organizations, the first interview may be with a member of the human resources department to determine if the applicant is qualified. Subsequent interviews are likely to be with the staff member for whom the job seeker will be working. For example, a teacher applying for a job in a large school district is likely to interview with the human resources director first, and then, if this interview goes well, with the principal of the school where the teacher would be working. On the other hand, an applicant for a job at a small child care center will probably interview directly with the director of the center.

The first part of every interview is devoted to breaking the ice and establishing rapport. Even clichés about the weather may be exchanged. Frequently, the interviewer opens with a comment about activities mentioned in the interviewee's résumé, especially if one is a bit out of the ordinary, such as playing polo.

The heart of the interview occurs when applicants describe their qualifications in answer to questions from the interviewer. Interviewees should always listen very attentively to questions and should avoid negative comments and exaggerations. This is also the time to ask any questions the applicant has. These questions should be about work-related activities. It is inappropriate to ask about salaries and benefits until after a job has been offered. At the end of the interview, the job seeker should always express appreciation for the interview and ask for the job.

FOCUSING ON THE FUTURE

Once a job has been offered and accepted, job seekers who want to be involved with children are ready to start or continue careers that will bring them satisfaction. No matter what their careers are, they will receive smiles and hugs from little children and quiet or boisterous appreciation from older children. And it is not only the children who will applaud their work: the children's parents will, too. In fact, North American society holds in great esteem those individuals who devote their lives to working with children.

APPENDIX: SOURCES OF ADDITIONAL INFORMATION

This section lists names, addresses, and websites of associations and other organizations that provide useful career information. By contacting these groups, individuals can find out about what specific careers are like, preparation needed for careers, typical salaries, job opportunities, and more.

CHAPTER 3: WORKING IN CHILD CARE CENTERS

Canadian Child Care
    Federation
201–383 Parkdale Avenue
Ottawa, ON K1Y 4R4
cccf-fcsge.ca

Center for the Child Care
    Workforce
555 New Jersey Avenue NW
Washington, DC 20001
ccw.org

Child Care Resource and Research
    Center
University of Toronto
455 Spadina Avenue,
    Suite 305
Toronto, ON M5S 2G8
childcarecanada.org

Council for Early Childhood
    Professional Recognition
    (CECPR)
2460 16th Street NW
Washington, DC 2000-35759
cdacouncil.org

National AfterSchool Association
529 Main Street, Suite 214
Charlestown, MA 02129
naaweb.org

National Association of Child Care
    Professionals
304–A Roanoke Street
Christiansburg, VA 24073
naccp.org

National Child Care Association
    (NCCA)
2025 M Street NW,Suite 800
Washington, DC 20036-3309
nccanet.org

National Child Care Information
    Center
10530 Rosehaven Street,
    Suite 400
Fairfax, VA 22030
nccic.org

CHAPTER 4: CARING FOR CHILDREN IN YOUR HOME

Canadian Child Care Federation
201–383 Parkdale Avenue
Ottawa, ON K1Y 4R4
cccf-fcsge.ca

Food and Nutrition Service
3101 Park Center Drive
Alexandria, VA 22303
fns.usda.gov

National Association for Family
    Child Care
5202 Pinemont Drive
Salt Lake City, UT 84123
nafcc.org

National Association of Child Care
    Resource and Referral Agencies
    (NACCRRA)
3101 Wilson Boulevard, Suite 350
Arlington, VA 22201
naccrra.org

National Resource Center for
    Health and Safety in Child Care
    and Early Education
UCHSC at Fitzsimons
Campus Mail Stop F541;
    P.O. Box 6508
Aurora, CO 80045-0508
http://nrc.uchsc.edu

CHAPTER 5: WORKING AS A NANNY

Canadian Nanny Association
1185 Eglinton Avenue East,
    Suite 701
Toronto, ON M3C 3C6
nanny1.org

International Nanny Association
    (INA)
2020 Southwest Freeway, Suite 208
Houston, TX 77098
nanny.org

National Alliance of Professional
Nanny Agencies
1071 Founders Boulevard, Suite A
Athens, GA 30606
theapna.org

National Association
for Nanny Care
Box 34783
Bethesda, MD 20827
nannycredential.org

CHAPTER 6: WORKING AS A BABYSITTER

American Red Cross National
Headquarters (ARC)
8111 Gatehouse Road
Falls Church, VA 22042
redcross.org

Canada Safety Council
1020 Thomas Spratt Place
Ottawa, ON K1G 5L5
safety-council.org

Canadian Red Cross
170 Metcalfe Street, Suite 300
Ottawa, ON K1G 5L5
redcross.ca

U.S. Consumer Product Safety
Commission
Eastern Regional Center
4330 East West Highway
Bethesda, MD 20814
cpsc.gov

Safe Sitter, Inc.
8604 Allisonville Road,
Suite 248
Indianapolis, IN 46250-1597
safesitter.org

CHAPTER 7: EDUCATING CHILDREN

American Federation of Teachers
555 New Jersey Avenue NW
Washington, DC 20001
aft.org

American Montessori Society
281 Park Avenue S.,
6th Floor
New York, NY 10010
amshq.org

Canadian Association of
Montessori Teachers
1 Banigan Drive
Toronto, ON M4H 1G3
camt.ca

Canadian Teachers' Federation
2490 Don Reid Drive
Ottawa, ON K1G 5L5
ctf-fce.ca

Council for Professional
Recognition
1460 16th Street NW
Washington, DC 20036
cdacouncil.org

National Association for the
Education of Young Children
(NAEYC)
1509 16th Street NW
Washington, DC 20036
naeyc.org

National Board for Professional
Teaching Standards
1525 Wilson Boulevard, Suite 500
Arlington, VA 22209
nbpts.org

National Council for
Accreditation of Teacher
Education
2010 Massachusetts Avenue NW,
Suite 500
Washington, DC 20036-1023
ncate.org

National Education Association
(NEA)
1201 16th Street NW
Washington, DC 20036-3290
nea.org

National Head Start Association
1651 Prince Street
Alexandria, VA 22314
nhsa.org

Recruiting New Teachers, Inc.
385 Concord Avenue, Suite 103
Belmont, MA 02478
recruitingteachers.org

CHAPTER 8: WORKING WITH CHILDREN IN SPORTS AND RECREATION CAREERS

Sports

Coaching Association
of Canada
141 Laurier Avenue West, Suite 300
Ottawa, ON K1P 5J3
coach.ca

National Alliance
for Youth Sports
2050 Vista Parkway
West Palm Beach, FL 33411-2718
nays.org

National Association
for Girls and Women in Sport
(NAGWS)
1900 Association Drive
Reston, VA 22091
aahperd.org

National Association for Sport and
Physical Education
1900 Association Drive
Reston, VA 22091
aahperd.org

National Council of Athletic
Training
1900 Association Drive
Reston, VA 22091
aahperd.org

Tennis Canada
Rexall Centre
1 Shoreham Drive, Suite 100
Toronto, ON M3N 3A6
tenniscanada.com

U.S. Professional Tennis Association
353 Briarpark Drive, Suite One
Houston, TX 77042
uspta.org

United States Tennis Association
70 West Red Oak Lane
White Plains, NY 10604
usta.com

Recreation

American Alliance for Health,
    Physical Education, Recreation,
    and Dance (AAHPERD)
1900 Association Drive
Reston, VA 22091
aahperd.org

American Association for Leisure
    and Recreation (AALR)
1900 Association Drive
Reston, VA 22091
aahperd.org

American Camping Association
Bradford Woods
5000 State Road, 67 North
Martinsville, IN 46151-7902
acacamps.org

Canadian Association
    for Health, Physical
    Education, Recreation, and
    Dance
301–2197 Riverside Drive
Ottawa, ON K1H 7X3
cahperd.ca

Canadian Camping
    Association
2494 Rte. 125 Sud
St-Donat, QC J0T 2C0
ccamping.org

Canadian Parks and Recreation
    Association
404–2197 Riverside Drive
Ottawa, ON K1H 7X3
ccamping.org

National Employee Services and
    Recreation Association
2211 York Road, Suite 207
Oak Brook, IL 60521-2371
esmassn.org

National Recreation and Park
    Association
22377 Belmont Ridge Road
Ashburn, VA 20148-4501
nrpa.org

YMCA of the USA
101 North Wacker Drive
Chicago, IL 60606
ymca.net

YMCA Canada
42 Charles Street East, 6th floor
Toronto, ON M4Y 1T4
ymca.ca

CHAPTER 9: KEEPING CHILDREN HEALTHY

General

American Dental Association
211 East Chicago Avenue, Suite 1814
Chicago, IL 60611-2678
ada.org

American Dental Hygienists
    Association
444 North Michigan Avenue,
    Suite 3400
Chicago, IL 60611
adha.org

American Medical Association
515 North State Street
Chicago, IL 60610-4377
ama-assn.org

American Nurses Association
8515 Georgia Avenue, Suite 400
Silver Spring, MD 20910
nursingworld.org

Association of American Medical
    Colleges
Section for Student Services
2450 N Street NW
Washington, DC 20037-1131
aamc.org

Canadian Dental Association
1815 Alta Vista Drive
Ottawa, ON K1G 3YB
cda-adc.ca

Canadian Dental Hygienists
    Association
96 Centrepointe Drive
Ottawa, ON K2G 6B1
cdha.ca

Canadian Federation of Medical
    Students National Office
130 Slater Street, Suite 750
Ottawa, ON K1P6E2
cdha.ca

Canadian Medical Association
1867 Alta Vista Drive
Ottawa, ON K1G 3Y6
cma.ca

Canadian Nurses Association
50 Driveway
Ottawa, ON K2P 1E2
cna-nurses.ca

National League for Nursing
61 Broadway, 33rd Floor
New York, NY 10006
nln.org

Pediatric Medicine

American Academy of Pediatric
    Dentistry
211 East Chicago Avenue, Suite 700
Chicago, IL 60611-2616
aapd.org

American Academy
    of Pediatrics
141 Northwest Point Boulevard
P.O. Box 927
Elk Grove Village, IL 60009-0927
aap.org

American Society of Dentistry
    for Children (ASDC)
875 North Michigan Avenue,
    Suite 4040
Chicago, IL 60611
ucsf.edu/ads/asdc

Association for the Care of
    Children's Health (ACCH)
19 Mantau Road
Mount Royal, NJ 08061
acch.org

Canadian Paediatric Society
50 Driveway
Ottawa, ON K1G 4J8
cps.ca

National Association of
    Children's Hospitals and
    Related Institutions
401 Wythe Street
Alexandria, VA 22314
childrenshospitals.net

National Association of Pediatric
    Nurse Associates and
    Practitioners (NAPNAP)
1101 Kings Highway N., Suite 206
Cherry Hill, NJ 08034-1931
napnap.org

American Academy of Child and
    Adolescent Psychiatry
    (AACAP)
3615 Wisconsin Avenue NW
Washington, DC 20016-3007
aacap.org

American Association of
    Children's Residential Centers
11700 W. Lake Park Drive
Milwaukee, WI 53224
aacre-dc.org

American Association of
    Psychiatric Services for
    Children
220 Hibiscus Drive
Rochester, NY 14618
apa.org

American Counseling Association
5999 Stevenson Avenue
Alexandria, VA 22304-3300
counseling.org

American Psychiatric Association
    (APA)
1000 Wilson Boulevard, Suite 1825
Alexandria, VA 22209-3901
psych.org

American Psychological
    Association
750 1st Street NE
Washington, DC 20002-4242
apa.org

American School Counselors
   Association
1101 King Street, Suite 625
Alexandria, VA 22314
schoolcounselor.org

Canadian Counseling Association
16 Concourse Gate, Suite 600
Ottawa, ON K2E 7S8
ccacc.ca

Canadian Psychiatric Association
141 Laurier Avenue West,
   Suite 701
Ottawa, ON K1P 5J3
cpa-apc.org

Canadian Psychological
   Association
141 Laurier Avenue West, Suite 702
Ottawa, ON K1P 5J3
cpa-cpa.ca

Child Life Council, Inc.
11820 Parklawn Drive,
   Suite 240
Rockville, MD 20852
childlife.org

Speech-Language Pathology

American Speech-Language-
   Hearing Association
10801 Rockville Pike
Rockville, MD 20852
asha.org

Canadian Association of Speech
   Language Pathologists
920–1 Nicholas Street
Ottawa, ON K1P 5J3
caslpa.ca

CHAPTER 10: ENSURING THE WELFARE OF CHILDREN

Social Workers

Big Brothers Big Sisters
   of America (BBBSA)
230 North 13th Street
Philadelphia, PA 19107
bbs.org

Big Brothers Big Sisters of Canada
3228 South Service Road, Suite 113E
Curlington, ON L7N 3H8
bbbs.ca

Boys and Girls Clubs of America
1275 Peachtree Street NE
Atlanta, GA 30309-5700
bgca.org

Boys and Girls Clubs of Canada
7100 Woodbine Avenue, Suite 405
Markham, ON L3R 5J2
bgccan.com

Canadian Association for Schools
   of Social Work
1398 ch. Star Top Road
Ottawa, ON K1B 4V7
casw-acts.ca

Canadian Association of Social
  Workers
383 Parkdale Avenue
Ottawa, ON K1Y 4R4
casw-acts.ca

Child Welfare League of America
  (CWLA)
440 1st Street NW, Suite 310
Washington, DC 20001
cwla.org

Council on Social Work Education
1600 Duke Street
Alexandria, VA 22314-3421
cswe.org

National Association of School
  Psychologists
4030 East West Highway,
  Suite 402
Bethesda, MD 20814
nasponline.org

National Association of Social
  Workers
750 1st Street NE,
  Suite 700
Washington, DC 20002-4241
naswdc.org

National Committee to Prevent
  Child Abuse
332 South Michigan Avenue,
  Suite 1600
Chicago, IL 60604-4357
childabuse.org

Police Officers

Canadian Police College
P.O. Box 8900
Ottawa, ON K1G 3J2
cpc.gc.ca

International Juvenile Officers
  Association
59 7th Street
Garden City Park, NY 11040
it.ojp.gov

Juvenile Justice

American Bar Association, Young
  Lawyers Division
750 North Lake Shore Drive
Chicago, IL 60611-6281
abanet.org/yld

American Judges Association
National Center for State Courts
300 Newport Avenue
Williamsburg, VA 23187-8798
aja.ncs.dni.us

Canadian Bar Association
500–825 Carling Avenue
Ottawa, ON K1S 5S8
cba.org

National Council of Juvenile
  and Family Court Judges
University of Nevada
P.O. Box 8970
Reno, NV 89507
ncjfcj.org

National Court Appointed
   Special Advocate Association
100 West Harrison Street,
   No. 500
Seattle, WA 98119
nationalcasa.org

CHAPTER 11: INTRODUCING CHILDREN TO THE WORLD OF ARTS AND ENTERTAINMENT

Art Teachers

National Art Education
   Association (U.S. and
   Canada)
1916 Association Drive
Reston, VA 22091-1590
naea-reston.org

Children's Artists

Allied Artists of America
15 Gramercy Park South
New York, NY 10003
alliedartistsofamerica.org

The American Institute
   of Graphic Arts
164 5th Avenue
New York, NY 10010
aiga.org

Society of Illustrators
128 East 63rd Street
New York, NY 10021
societyillustrators.org

Music Teachers

National Association for Music
   Education (MENC)
1806 Robert Fulton
Reston, VA 20190
menc.org

National Association of Schools
   of Music
11250 Roger Bacon Drive,
   Suite 21
Reston, VA 22091
nasm.arts-accredit.org

Dance Teachers

American Dance Therapy
   Association
2000 Century Plaza, Suite 108
10632 Little Patuxent Parkway
Columbia, MD 21044
adta.org

Canadian Dance Teachers
   Association
6033 Shawson Drive, Unit 38
Mississauga, ON L5T 1H8
cdtaont.com

Dance Educators
    of America
Box 607
Pelham, NY 10803-0607
deadance.com

National Association of Schools
    of Dance (NASD)
11250 Roger Bacon Drive,
    Suite 21
Reston, VA 22091
nasd.arts-accredit.org

National Dance Association
1900 Association Drive
Reston, VA 20191
aahperd.org/nda

Books

Canadian Society of Children's
    Authors, Illustrators, and
    Performers
104–40 Orchard View
    Boulevard
Lower Level Entrance
Toronto, ON M4R 1B9
canscaip.org

Society of Children's Book
    Writers and Illustrators
8271 Beverly Boulevard
Los Angeles, CA 90048
scwbi.org

Magicians

Canadian Association
    of Magicians
Box 41
Elora, ON N0B 1S0
canadianassociationofmagicians.com

International Brotherhood
    of Magicians
11137 South Towne Square
St. Louis, MO 63123
magician.org

Clowns

Clowns of America,
    International
P.O. Box 6468
Lees Summit, MO 64064
coai.org

World Clown Association
    (U.S. and Canada)
worldclownassociation.com

Children's Television Shows

Canadian Association
    of Broadcasters
P.O. Box 627, Stn. B
Ottawa, ON K1P 5S2
cab-acr.ca

National Association
    of Broadcasters
1771 N Street NW
Washington, DC 20036
nab.org

CHAPTER 12: ADDITIONAL CAREERS WORKING WITH CHILDREN

Children's Librarians

Association for Library Service
    to Children
American Library Association
50 East Huron Street
Chicago, IL 60611
ala.org/alsc

Canadian Library Association
328 Frank Street
Ottawa, ON K2P 0X8
cla.ca

Children's Photographers

Professional Photographers
    of America, Inc.
57 Forsyth Street, Suite 1600
Atlanta, GA 30303
ppa.com

Professional Photographers
    of Canada
ppoc.ca

Children's Museums

American Association
    of Museums
1575 I Street NW,
    Suite 400
Washington, DC 20005
aam-us.org

Association of Children's
    Museums (U.S. and Canada)
1300 L Street NW,
    Suite 975
Washington, DC 20005
childrensmuseums.org

Association of Youth Museums
1775 K Street NW,
    Suite 595
Washington, DC 20006
aym.org

Religious Workers

Canadian Council
    of Churches
47 Queen's Park Crescent East
Toronto, ON M5S 2C3
ccc-cce.ca

National Council of Churches
Professional Church Leadership,
    Room 863
475 Riverside Drive
New York, NY 10115
nccusa.org

Creating Products for Children

Canadian Toy Association
7777 Keele Street, Suite 212
Concord, ON L4K 1Y7
cdntoyassn.com

National Retail Federation
327 7th Street NW, Suite 1000
Washington, DC 20004
nrf.com

Retail Council of Canada
1255 Bay Street, Suite 800
Toronto, ON M5R 2A9
retailcouncil.org

Toy Manufacturers of America
1115 Broadway, Suite 400
New York, NY 10010
toy-tia.org

More Jobs

AmeriCorps
1201 New York Avenue NW
Washington, DC 20525
americorps.org

Peace Corps of the United States
1111 20th Street NW
Washington, DC 20526
peacecorps.gov

United Nations Children's Fund
(UNICEF)
3 United Nations Plaza
New York, NY 10017
unicef.org

Voluntary Service Overseas
806–151 Slater Street
Ottawa, ON K1P 5H3
vsocan.org

CHAPTER 13: SEARCHING FOR A JOB WORKING WITH CHILDREN

United States and Canada

The Riley Guide: Employment Opportunities and Job Resources on the Internet
rileyguide.com

Canada

Canadian Job Website Directory
jobpostcanada.com

United States

Monstertrak
monstertrak.monster.com

ABOUT THE AUTHORS

Marjorie Eberts is a professional author who writes in the areas of careers and education. She holds an M.A. in education from Stanford University and an education specialist degree from Butler University. Her expertise in child care has evolved from ten years of experience as a teacher along with work as a supervisor of a university reading center for children.

Margaret Gisler is a professional author and an expert in the field of child care. She has taught preschool, kindergarten, and first grade. In addition, she has been a college instructor of reading and a supervisor of a reading clinic for children. For more than six years, Margaret worked with children as a camp counselor, lifeguard, fitness instructor, and waterfront director. Her educational background includes a doctorate and master's degree in education from Ball State University and an education specialist degree from Butler University.

Together, the two authors have written more than eighty books, predominantly in the field of careers and education. They have published several books for children, including a series of books on phonics and a book that teaches nutrition and shapes to preschoolers. The two authors have also written books that help parents prepare young children for school and help students learn study skills. Recently, they have written several supplementary reading programs for elementary school children. In addition, they write a nationally syndicated newspaper column, "Dear Teacher," which gives advice to parents on how they can help their children succeed in school.

As the mothers of six children between them, the authors have gained firsthand experience with many professionals in the child care arena. Through their children they have been involved with teachers, tutors, coaches, camp counselors, pediatricians, pediatric dentists and nurses, private music teachers, counselors, speech therapists, children's librarians, youth ministers, babysitters, and child care center owners and workers as well as home-based child care providers.